M000040158

SILVER SPOON

To Antwone
and Kavonte

Find your Silver Spoon!

SILVER SPOON

THE *IMPERFECT* GUIDE to SUCCESS

BENNIE FOWLER

LIONCREST
PUBLISHING

COPYRIGHT © 2019 BENNIE FOWLER
All rights reserved.

SILVER SPOON
The Imperfect Guide to Success

ISBN   978-1-5445-0476-6 *Hardcover*
         978-1-5445-0477-3 *Paperback*
         978-1-5445-0478-0 *Ebook*

Dedicated to my brother, Chris Fowler.

CONTENTS

FOREWORD

THE MIND OF A WINNER

Most people struggle with being honest with themselves.

Bennie Fowler is not most people.

He knows exactly who he is, and what he's all about.

I've known Bennie a long time—a lifetime, really. When we were young, we all loved basketball. We had hoop dreams. But as much as Bennie loved basketball, he knew from a young age there were things he could do on a football field that other players could only dream of. He was really good at basketball. He was *amazing* at football. Those skills drove him to become an all-state wide receiver, then to success at Michigan State, and now to shine as a star player in the NFL.

Bennie was honest with himself. He knew his strengths and his gifts, and his success is no surprise to anyone who knows him. He knew if he focused his energies on football, he'd become one of the best to ever play the game. And as hard as he worked on physical conditioning and becoming an elite athlete, he also put in the mental work to reach his full potential.

He was hungry. He still is. One of the things that makes Bennie so interesting is the journey he took to get to where he is, and that's a journey readers take with him in this book. But this book not only takes readers by the hand and shows them the life and times of Bennie Fowler, it also lays out the attitude, work ethic, and intellectual strength Bennie used to become a winner, both on and off the field.

Everyone knows Bennie Fowler, the Super Bowl champion—but let's look at what got him there. He had great parents who were well-off, but no one ever handed Bennie anything. His parents made him work for everything he got, and he worked hard. He faced the challenges life presented and crushed them, earning spots as a top-tier football player, brilliant athlete, and all-around good guy. He has succeeded on the football field and in life through hard work, perseverance, and strong mental conditioning.

It's incredibly hard to move Bennie off his center. He's

always happy, always in a good mood—just a hard-working, smart, fun guy to be around. That's because Bennie spends as much time working on his mental game as he does his physical game.

Read this book and get insight into the mind of a champion—a guy who has worked hard every day of his life and knows what it takes to win. Whether you're a professional athlete, brand-new to the workforce, or just need more focus and determination in your life, there's something in this book for you. So get ready to meet a man who will change your life. Bennie Fowler—I'm proud of this book he's written and even prouder to call him my friend.

DRAYMOND GREEN

INTRODUCTION

PEYTON'S LAST PASS

Super Bowl 50.

The third most-watched program in American television history.

Over 110 million people were tuned in when my team, the Denver Broncos, squared off against the Carolina Panthers in Levi's Stadium in Santa Clara, California. The sidelines were thick with former NFL stars on hand to mark the fiftieth anniversary of this championship game, and the stands were packed with more than seventy thousand fans.

Can you say *pressure?*

Carolina was a tough team. They'd gone 15–1 and their quarterback, Cam Newton, was the league's MVP. Newton, in the eyes of some, looked invincible.

My team, on the other hand, was led by the oldest quarterback to start a Super Bowl—thirty-nine-year-old Peyton Manning. Peyton missed several games during the regular season with a foot injury. He led the league in interceptions and was having his worst season since his rookie year in 1998. Peyton, for the first time in his illustrious career, had been benched earlier in the year but had worked his way back into the lineup toward the end of the regular season.

Still, thanks in large part to our defense, we were leading 16–10 when Carolina got the ball near their own twenty-yard line with four minutes left. Anyone who's watched an NFL game knows that this did not make us feel overconfident. Newton had plenty of time and talent to mount a drive that would allow Carolina to take the lead.

Then, on third and nine, Newton dropped back to pass, and our great linebacker, Von Miller, swept in and stripped the ball as Newton was beginning his throw. The ball bobbled around before our safety, T.J. Ward, fell on it a few yards from the Carolina end zone. A few plays later, running back C.J. Anderson plunged in from two yards out for the touchdown, and we were up 22–10.

While most of us celebrated, our coaches were urgently talking into their headsets. Kick the extra point? Or go for the two-point conversion?

If we kicked the extra point, we'd be up by thirteen points. But there was still time left for Carolina to storm back. If the Panthers could get a quick score and get the ball back on an onside kick or a turnover, they could still win the game 24–23 with a second touchdown.

Head Coach Gary Kubiak elected to go for the two-point conversion, which would put us ahead 24–10 and keep us in the game even if Carolina came back in the final minutes.

Here comes Bennie Fowler.

WHY I'M WRITING THIS BOOK

As I trotted out onto the field with Peyton and the rest of the offensive unit amid the stadium roar, I felt one dominant sensation:

Joy.

I knew the play because I'd practiced it over and over. I knew where the ball would arrive because I'd visualized this moment over and over. I could picture the spinning laces as Peyton's spiral cut through the air. I could see it sailing into my hands, and I could feel it slamming into my gut as I came out of my break. My mind was quiet and focused because I had learned to fill it with positive thoughts and flush out any feelings of self-doubt or fear.

People think of NFL players and other professional athletes as great physical specimens—and they are. Look at my former teammate Demaryius Thomas—he's tall, muscled, runs like a deer, and has fluid moves that leave most defenders flailing.

But what people often don't realize is how much mental work goes into being a professional athlete. The best ones—the Peyton Mannings, the Kobe Bryants, the Von Millers, the Draymond Greens (well, there really is only *one* Draymond Green)—are towers of mental strength too. They have the powers of perseverance, patience, and discipline, and they have trained their minds as finely as they have honed their physical skills.

They train their minds by following simple principles and practices. They close out negative thoughts while cultivating rich, prosperous ideas. They focus on the things they can control, and as they gain mastery over those factors, any sense of anxiety fades away. Their heart rate goes down, their breathing is relaxed, their muscles are loose, and their thoughts are clear and precise.

These are skills I've learned in my five years in the NFL, but they are skills anyone can master. When you focus on what my mentor and friend Dr. Rick Perea calls "the process," your performance improves. Who among us wouldn't benefit from becoming healthier, calmer, more confident, and successful?

Focusing on the process allowed me to smile to myself as I prepared to receive the biggest pass of my career from a future Hall of Famer throwing the last pass of his career.

THE LAST PASS—AND THE BEGINNING OF SOMETHING BIG

The play is called scat and vertigo. It's not always designed to go to me, but on this occasion, I knew it was. In the huddle, Peyton looked me in the eye.

"Just give me a little time to find the laces," he said in that now-all-too-familiar Southern drawl of his. Since his retirement, Peyton has come to be known through his commercials as a sort of goofy optimist who thinks he can write country songs better than Brad Paisley. But make no mistake—Peyton Manning is smart, intense, competitive, and anything but a hayseed.

I approached the line of scrimmage and spread out wide to Peyton's right. As he barked out the signals, he looked to his left and then to his right, locking his eyes on mine for a split second. I raised my hand slightly, letting him know that the coverage was what we expected and that I was ready. Suddenly, the field exploded with twenty-two men bolting upright and slamming into each other in a wild flurry of grunts and shouts.

It was a beautiful ballet of violence, inch-perfect in its choreography. I was joyous.

Peyton dropped back two steps as I raced for the end zone. The ball arrived as I came out of my break, smacking into my gut as my arms folded around it. I tumbled, rolled twice, and then popped back to my feet, holding the ball aloft. My teammates bunched around me, slapping my helmet.

I danced like everybody was watching, holding the ball tight.

SOMETHING DIFFERENT

I didn't write this book to speak only to athletes. Therefore, don't put this book down just because there's an athlete on the cover. I wrote this book to share universal human experiences, aspects of life everyone can see themselves in. No matter who you are, every part of what you do well, every part of what you're passionate about, requires the will, determination, and mental fortitude honed by great athletes in moments of immense pressure.

Now, if you happen to be a football fan, this book might be a revelation to you; it's definitely different than most books by professional athletes.

This won't be a blow-by-blow account of playing with Peyton (or later with his brother, Eli).

Still, you'll hear from plenty of athletes. Rick Perea was an NFL linebacker before he became a sports psychologist. Julius Thomas was a Denver tight end and is now working on his doctorate in psychology. Seth Minter, aka "The Foot Doctor," made a name for himself as a genius-level footwork trainer for some of the best running backs and wide receivers in the NFL.

You'll also hear from others—my good friend Draymond; Desyree Thomas, a former women's basketball star who now owns her own menswear brand; and Marell Evans, a great football player who is now a venture capitalist in the San Francisco Bay Area. You'll hear from my brother, who endured seven knee surgeries but never wavered in his commitment to basketball. You'll hear from my dad, one of the best coaches I ever had, and from my mother, whose instincts helped lead me to football.

Each of these people has a mind like tempered steel and has helped me forge my own resilience. They helped me realize that habits and attitudes contribute as much to a person's success as weight training and drills.

This book won't teach you to bench 250 pounds or run a 4.4 in the forty-yard dash. Instead, it will share insights I've developed for overcoming adversity, staying focused, and persevering to achieve dreams and goals. I'll explore the mental and personal characteristics that successful athletes embrace but which can also help you clear your own path to success.

Athletes are not superhuman, but many do have profound ideas and approaches to mental strength. The best players work to get better every day, regardless of the obstacles they encounter. What sets them apart is their determination and resilience—their ability to bounce back and see past the day-to-day setbacks we all encounter.

I want my story, and the stories my friends will tell in this book, to inspire you to say:

> I'm going to do what I want to do. I'm going to achieve what I want to achieve.

Sports is a business—no one knows this better than an NFL player—but it's also a game. We play sports for fun, right? That's the way it should be. Fun should be your life, my mom always said.

But my mother also had other things to say about fun and games.

"Work before you play and all your life you will thrive," she always told my brother and me. "You can't just go out there and have fun all the time. You have to put in the work. The work is what makes fun and games so enjoyable."

THINGS YOU NEED TO HEAR

I'm calling this book *Silver Spoon: The Imperfect Guide to Success* because I want to debunk the notion that well-to-do people don't face discouraging setbacks or adversity. They do. I grew up in a suburb of Detroit, the son of an attorney and an auto executive, and I went to a private prep school before heading to Michigan State on a football scholarship. We were able to pay our bills and live well. It's not the typical rags-to-riches narrative that's often celebrated in our society, nor is it the story of a trust fund kid out of Beverly Hills, but that doesn't make what I will speak to you about here any less important, or, for that matter, any less thrilling.

Nor does it mean that my parents coddled my brother,

Chris, and me, or that we've never faced daunting challenges. Far from it.

Our parents never suggested we could afford to back down or take an easier path. They've always challenged us to be better—better people, better learners, better athletes. When at age ten, my brother tore the ACL in his right leg, my mother did not indulge his disappointment. Instead, she told him that he needed to learn how to drive left and develop new strengths. I was a basketball player too, but when I ran a 10.9 in the hundred meters in high school, my mother told me that kind of speed would help me more on a football field than on a basketball court.

That's my mom. She was never harsh, but she was always honest. She told you things you didn't necessarily *want* to hear, but they were things you *needed* to know. Neither she nor my dad felt the need to make Chris and me improved versions of themselves. Instead, they wanted us to be improved versions of *ourselves*.

"I gave myself the freedom to see who you boys were as opposed to seeing myself or your dad in you," she told me recently when we were talking about this book. "I insisted that you be the best at what you *are* best at."

And now I'm insisting that you do the same thing.

Read on to find out just how rewarding that process can be.

CHAPTER ONE

ADVERSITY COMES FOR EVERYONE

"Perhaps I lost sight of my dreams when I became an adult and resigned myself to acting the way adults are supposed to act. Maybe I lost sight of them when I went to law school and started talking like lawyers were supposed to talk. In any event, that evening...made me resolve to stop spending so much time making a living and to spend far more time creating a life."

ROBIN SHARMA, *THE MONK WHO SOLD HIS FERRARI*

In March of 1999, I became extremely sad in my second-grade homeroom class. Not understanding the sudden crush of this emotion, I began to cry. I was inconsolable.

Two months prior, my mom, my younger brother Chris,

and I moved from our house in Farmington Hills, Michigan, to a condo in downtown Detroit. My parents had explained that we would be living apart from my dad, but since my dad had previously lived and worked apart from us in London, Ontario, for a while and often traveled for work, the eventual permanence of this living arrangement did not immediately resonate with me. Even after we moved to downtown Detroit, I saw my dad almost every day at track or basketball practice and every weekend.

That day in March, my teacher called my mom after she unsuccessfully tried to calm me down. I explained to her my mom and dad were not living together anymore. My parents had not shared the news of their divorce with anyone outside the family. But somehow, at that moment, my life was different. All that had been normal to me was gone in an instant.

My mom let me cry, and she cried with me. She apologized for the difficulty and made chocolate chip cookies (the kind you slice, not from scratch). Then, I did my homework and went to bed. I got up the next morning, got dressed, had breakfast, and went to school. After school, I went to practice. Both my parents always attended every practice for track, basketball, football, soccer, etc., and they were both there that day. My dad put the team through our regular warm-up, and we scrimmaged with another team. And this day was better than the day before.

The overwhelmingness of hurt sometimes changes patterns; returning to what works, works.

In 2012, in my junior year at Michigan State, our team was ranked thirteenth in the country. Many of our best players were returning, including Le'Veon Bell, our great running back.

We started the year strong, edging past twenty-fourth-ranked Boise State and then clobbering Central Michigan 41–7. When twentieth-ranked Notre Dame came to town on the evening of September 15, we were tenth in the country and feeling confident.

That confidence did not last. Notre Dame's defense smothered us, and we struggled to get first downs, let alone touchdowns. The Fighting Irish scored first, and at halftime, they led 14–3. The eighty thousand fans at Spartan Stadium and the ABC broadcasters in the booth wondered if we were going to show up in the second half.

We didn't. We were shut out in the second half in an ugly performance, and one of the ugliest performances came from me. Late in the game, I dropped an easy nineteen-yard toss that should have been a touchdown.

The massive groan that rose in the stadium as that pass slipped through my fingers was just the beginning. After the game, every reporter within a hundred square miles of the stadium wanted to know why I dropped the pass, what caused the drop, and how I felt about it. Social media blew up with accusations and recriminations as that dropped pass came to represent everything that had gone wrong for us that night.

This was the heaviest dose of adversity I'd ever encountered. I struggled with how to respond. Would the dropped pass define me as a player (*He's had some issues with drops*, the announcers would say)? Would it undercut my confidence? How could I push it from my mind when, for the next week on campus, everyone I passed seemed to be glaring at me—or worse yet, dropping their eyes? Just like in second grade, I experienced the overwhelmingness of hurt, coupled this time with embarrassment. Again, returning to what works, works.

I chose to use the dropped pass as motivation to work harder. I recalled my mom's actions when I cried over the divorce; I reminded myself that I was the starting wide receiver (the equivalent of chocolate chip cookies) on one of the best teams in the country. To get there, I'd worked my ass off. There had been countless early mornings and late nights, routes run over and over (the equivalent of doing my homework). None of that work had vanished. I was still the product of all that hard work. And I couldn't let one dropped pass erase that fact (just like my mom assuring me tomorrow would be better).

That moment, however, was a turning point. I could have become fearful or tentative. I could have started playing like I was more concerned about *dropping* the ball than *catching* it. When you think that way, it can become a self-fulfilling prophecy. You are looking for the threat of failure because you want to avoid it, and suddenly, that threat of failure is around every corner. In the Book of Job (3:25–26), the prophet recounts, "For the thing which I have greatly feared, has come upon me."

Some people may think that having a suburban upbringing was a "silver spoon" for me (translation: *he had it easy*), but I don't see it that way. To me, a true "silver spoon" is something you have that helps you succeed throughout your whole life. Something you didn't go out and earn—a free gift, like a coincidence of birth or circumstance over which you had no control—but is life changing all the same. Something that leaves such an indelible and positive mark on your life, you're a better person for it for the rest of your life. For me, my true silver spoon is the tradition of education, hard work, and perseverance my family practiced long before I came into the world, and instilled in me from the moment I was born. Adversity can help you find your true silver spoon. The only part of my upbringing that helped me to move past that dropped pass in college, and go on to catch the winning pass in the Super Bowl, was the hard work and perseverance I witnessed in my household daily. That was and is my silver spoon. Broadening my understanding of what makes a total athlete, and then becoming a more erudite student of the mental preparation necessary to overcome the adversity of a dropped pass, is how I use the gift of my silver spoon.

You might find your silver spoon after you tear your ACL, or they call you the third best in the office, or when you are denied second chair or that relished internship, or when you get cut or fired, or, worse yet, when you drop an easy pass on national television.

My silver spoon met adversity head-on and wasn't going to let it define or deflate me. Adversity would become my advocate, not my limiter. It would inspire me to new triumphs instead of allowing me to be complacent in the losses. Failure would motivate me to overcome adversity instead of convincing me to quit.

I kept it in perspective. It was one dropped pass. There would likely be others in my career. Instead of worrying about more drops, I focused on the good. I wanted the promise of future success surrounding me, not the dread of failure.

Live your life with fear and apprehension, and you will only find things to fear.

Live your life with joy and positivity, and you will find what you really want out of life.

I learned that the best approach is to stay focused on your goals and to keep working to reach them. I learned to treat failure as an opportunity to acquire new skills and knowledge.

Many of the players I admire think this way. Peyton Manning, for instance, acts like he doesn't have a care in the world. But he faced plenty of adversity the year I played with him. He had injuries that slowed him down. The media had documented a decline in the velocity of his passes after neck surgery earlier in his career. He wasn't as strong or as mobile as some of the younger quarterbacks. He was thirty-nine years old, when the average age of his teammates was twenty-five.

But Peyton never quit. He kept working. He found different ways to win that didn't require bullet passes and scrambling for extra yardage.

Quitting, he knew, could become a bad habit, and if you're not careful, it can become a destiny.

Peyton never quit, and I never quit. Quitting doesn't work. Don't do it.

HOW TO COPE WITH ADVERSITY

I wear a rubber bracelet in memory of a former teammate, punter Mike Sadler, who died in 2016 in a car crash while volunteering at a kicking camp in Wisconsin. Mike was only twenty-four when he died, but he'd already had a tremendous impact on the people around him. My Spartan teammates and I always thought Mike was on his way to becoming president of the United States. He had almost thirty thousand followers on Twitter, and his messages were always positive. He had six pillars to his philosophy:

- Get a good education.
- Set goals and aim high.
- Practice integrity and humility.
- Choose friends carefully.
- Share compassion with everyone.
- Find a reason to laugh each day.

The inscription on my bracelet says *The Prize is the Journey*. This reflects Mike's belief that the greatest reward in life is not our destination but the route we take to that destination. The prize is in the lessons we learn, the people we meet, and the little victories we enjoy along the way to reaching our most significant goals.

When I was playing for the Denver Broncos and we won Super Bowl 50, I was overcome with emotion the next day. I cried thinking about the game. I was ecstatic for the win. I was honored that I caught Peyton Manning's final NFL pass. These were all momentous achievements.

But none of those things were what brought me to tears.

I was brought to tears thinking of the path.

Of the journey.

That journey had as much adversity as joy, as much failure as success, as many setbacks as steps forward. And a dropped pass in 2012.

When I was in third grade, the teacher assigned everyone a book to read and write a report on. Now, what she *actually* assigned me was to read a few chapters of the first *Harry Potter* book. My parents and I misunderstood, though, and thought she wanted me to read the entire 300-plus-page book. I felt overwhelmed and a little angry; everyone else was assigned a book that was thirty or so pages, and here I was with hundreds of pages of Harry and his friends. There was no use complaining, though. This was my assignment (I thought), and I'd just have to buckle down and do it. After all, my parents weren't going to allow me any excuse.

Over the next three weeks, my parents and I devoted ourselves to getting me through this book. During lunch, I'd read a chapter. At dinner, my parents would help me read a chapter. In the car, we'd listen to a chapter of the audiobook or I'd read a chapter out loud. While my brother watched television and my friends played video games, I read Harry Potter. I even had to miss a couple basketball practices to finish the book on time. I really came to hate Harry Potter. But at the end of those three weeks, I had read a book no one in my class had even attempted and surprised the teacher with my report on the ENTIRE book. More than that, though, I had developed a habit of reading every day that has endured throughout my life. I never read any of the follow-up Harry Potter books, and to this day, I can't stand that one book I did read, but the experience of reading it made me a lifelong reader. It wasn't about the destination of reading that particular book; it was about the journey to becoming a disciplined learner.

That was one of my first concrete lessons in the power of a solid work ethic. It also taught me about the importance of attitude. I dreaded reading every single chapter of that assignment, but I learned if you approach everything with drudgery and pessimism, that is what your life becomes. And living in a constant cycle of dread and regret is not productive. This literary journey influenced many aspects of my life, including how I approached football and basketball and how I pursued my degree in economics, and taught me how to overcome adversity through discipline.

Everyone faces adversity at some point. Life is about ebbs and flows. It's not a steady state of bliss. It's filled with trial and error (and trial again). When that adversity arrives, here are some things to keep in mind:

- **Keep working.** Football taught me this, of course, because a whole lot of difficulty can come your way in football, even when you win. Losses (and dropped passes) are the worst, but not if you use those setbacks to redouble your efforts.
- **Have patience.** When I got cut by Chicago in 2018, I realized my football career wasn't going to progress according to my preferred timeline. There are too many things you can't control, so I learned to focus on the things I had power over and have patience with the things I didn't.
- **Practice what you're weak at.** This may sound obvious to some people. Still, I've watched many athletes become more complete players by focusing on their shortcomings.
- **Think positively.** The power of positive thinking is not a new idea, but it bears repeating. When you think about success and the things you're grateful for, little victories emerge, like mushrooms in a damp forest.
- **The adversity isn't the failure. The failure is let-**

ting trouble get the upper hand. One of my biggest disappointments was not getting drafted by the pros. But I never considered quitting. The failure wasn't in not getting selected. The failure would have been not trying to make the pros.

STRENGTH IN NUMBERS

When I signed with Chicago, I got a nice signing bonus, and everything was going well. I signed a one-year contract and had a good training camp. Then I got the call at the end of camp telling me I'd been cut. NFL teams all cut their rosters from 100 players to fifty-three players in one day, and I was one of the forty-seven players sent home that day. Here, I had to make another decision about my football life.

Then I got a text from my brother.

"Remember this feeling and how you feel right now," he said.

Then I got a text from my friend, Marell Evans.

"Good morning, bro," he wrote. "Just wanted to hit you up and say, 'Stay focused.' Keep grinding."

Then, Draymond.

"All made men been through some adversity," he wrote. "Now go make yourself."

TERESA GUEYSER, BENNIE'S MOTHER

Bennie and his friends were all comfortable playing basketball. They played together for years, and they all agreed to make basketball their career.

However, there are going to be times when people tell you the truth, and you don't want to hear it. When he was a sophomore in high school, Bennie ran a 10.9-second hundred-meter dash, and I said, "There's no way you can use that gift of speed on a basketball court. You're going to play football."

Football requires a different kind of work. You have to get hit, and you have to know what that means.

That's how [former NFL player and coach and current television analyst] Herm Edwards put it during a game I was watching on television. A wide receiver had been running a route over the middle. He decided to let the ball go rather than making the catch and possibly taking a big hit. Edwards said something like, "That guy made a business decision. Either I catch this ball and risk being knocked out of the game, or I let it go and live to let them throw me another one."

Although I encouraged him to play football, I also encouraged Bennie to see himself for what he was. Bennie loved basketball, loved to dunk the ball. He had major hops! That's why he was a state champion in the long jump in high school. But that was it for basketball: love, speed, and hops. Great gifts, but better maximized in a different venue.

I insisted that he be the best at the thing he was best at.

The point is that at a moment of profound disappointment, my support system cranked into gear and shored me up.

And the gist of each message was the same:

Persevere.

"Go make yourself," Draymond said.

Draymond has had a few instances of adversity in his career, and he'll tell you how important it is at those moments to have a support system.

"I don't care who you are, we all get to that point where we want to quit sometimes," he told me once. "It's our support system that keeps us going. It's our support system that gives us hope to know, 'Hey, you can do this. It didn't work out that time, but if you continue to push yourself, if you continue to work at whatever it is that you want to be great at or accomplish, you can do that.'"

For Draymond, that support flows in both directions. He gets support, but he also gives it. He gives it to me. He gives it to his mom. A key part of his motivation growing up was his mother. He'd seen her working three jobs, and he'd used that picture of his mom working hard as his motivation on the basketball court.

"On days that I didn't want to get out of bed and go to practice, I'd think, 'Well, my mother got up today to go to her three jobs. She's working for me. I need to work for her. I've got to get up. I've got to do my work so she doesn't have to do hers for the rest of her life.' That pushed me every single day."

It's paid off for Draymond. After he was drafted in the second round and signed a contract, he moved his mother out of what he called "the hood" and into a house in a better neighborhood. Three years later, when he signed his second contract, she was able to quit working altogether and hasn't worked since.

"That means everything to me," Draymond said.

RESOLVE

One of the main side effects of adversity is ambivalence. Ambivalence produces complacency and complacency produces quitting. As I said earlier, quitting, if not consciously averted, can become a destiny.

You can walk away.

Skip out on the struggle and the hard times.

For those who take that path, I'm sure there's a sweet release in just stopping and saying, "No more."

But "no more" could represent being totally consumed by that one thing that didn't quite work out right. "No more" could come to mean no movement or activity at all, when there is so much more that you can move or act on.

Just below every decision to move forward is a thick layer of doubt. Just below that is a layer of fear. And just below that is a measure of resolve. Resolve to be great, or resolve to just *be*.

That's why there are few character traits as fundamental to success and happiness as perseverance. You must be willing to show up every day and put your shoulder to the wheel. You must continue to battle no matter how much your mind, body, and spirit want to quit.

It's about persistence.

Tenacity.

It's dogged attention to your goals, and as we'll learn in the next chapter, it is a crucial element to your success.

CHAPTER TWO

PERSEVERANCE

"He conquers who conquers himself."

PUBLILIUS

"Our greatest weakness lies in giving up. The most certain way to success is to try just one more time."

THOMAS EDISON

I had every expectation of being an NFL Draft pick.

My agent and I felt I had the numbers to be selected as a wide receiver somewhere between the fourth and seventh rounds.

I'd excelled during my time as a Spartan. In addition to coming off a Big 10 Championship and victory in the 100th Rose Bowl, I led the team in receptions, yards, and touchdowns. I led the Big 10 in yards per reception, and battled through some early adversity—mostly injuries—to establish myself in my junior and senior seasons.

Being selected in the draft is every football player's dream. It guarantees you a shot at playing at the pinnacle of the sport.

It's a longshot for anyone, however. There are typically 2,000 seniors at Division I colleges and 3,500 players at Division II schools eligible for the draft each year. Still, only about 250 players are selected in the seven rounds of the draft. In the year I was eligible, NFL teams selected 256 players, including thirty-three wide receivers. The odds of anyone being selected are long, but I felt confident, and my agent felt optimistic too.

Then—Draft Day. We settled in to monitor the selection announcements and wait for a phone call from a coach or a general manager for one of the teams.

I didn't worry when I wasn't selected in the first few rounds. I hadn't expected my phone to ring that quickly. But as the rounds kept passing, I became anxious as my phone stayed silent.

In the last two rounds, six and seven, some NFL teams called but not with the news I had been selected. Instead, they called to see if I'd be interested in joining their organization as a free agent. The draft ended without my name being announced as a pick.

I want to tell you I took it in stride, but the truth is it hurt like hell. I was disappointed and a little pissed off. I'd sacrificed and worked hard for this opportunity and hated to see it slip away.

But the dream of playing in the NFL doesn't end for guys who aren't drafted. I still had the option of signing as a free agent. A lot of players actually prefer to go undrafted; the money they make can be similar to that of a late-round pick, and they can choose where they want to go. Not me: I wanted to hear my name called on national television. In the moment, I had forgotten my name had been announced on many prior occasions during nationally televised Spartan games, particularly the 2014 Rose Bowl. But that's what happens when you make it about the prize and not the journey.

In my case, the Detroit Lions offered me the most money. But I'd spent my entire life in Michigan and wanted to see some new sights, so I signed with the Denver Broncos. A change of scenery wasn't the only reason, however. I knew that by signing with Denver, I'd be catching passes thrown by Peyton Manning, one of the greatest quarterbacks to ever play the game. I also figured, if I could be successful in Denver with Peyton, I'd have the goods to play with anyone in the league.

It was too good an opportunity to pass up.

ONE DAY AT A TIME

In addition to Peyton, Denver also had veteran wide receivers like Demaryius Thomas, Julius Thomas, and Wes Welker. Wes had also been an undrafted free agent—in 2004—and had gone on to lead the league in receptions for three years (2007, 2009, and 2011) while playing for the New England Patriots. Learning my position from these guys was like getting a Harvard education on being an NFL receiver. In short order, the team also added Aqib Talib, Demarcus Ware, and T.J. Ward on defense, plus another amazing receiver in Emmanuel Sanders.

We were stacked, no doubt about it, and I eventually won a Super Bowl playing alongside these guys.

I took that first training camp in Denver one day at a time. I tried not to live too much in the future. I tried to learn and love every moment in that camp, and to take away as much knowledge as I could from the veterans around me. I didn't get caught up in worries about the future.

Despite this learning trajectory, I got more bad news at the end of camp: I'd been cut.

In the NFL, players who get cut during camp remain on the waiver wire for twenty-four hours and any team in the league can claim them. If that doesn't happen, your team can keep you on its practice squad, a reserve unit that acts in practice as the upcoming week's opponents. You draw a salary and are technically on the team, but it's a difficult existence. No waiver wire claim came, and I was signed to Denver's practice squad.

I endured tremendous uncertainty that season. There is no job security. The team can cut you whenever it wants or whenever it finds another player it likes better. You could be playing exceptionally well but if the team needs to stash a free agent on the squad, you could be cut in an instant.

It's precarious.

But I survived the season. Afterward, Julius Thomas took me under his wing and helped me improve as a player and as a person. Julius and I have similar personalities. After the season, he invited me to train with him in Los Angeles. It was a risky and expensive proposition, but I was all-in. I invested all my savings to work with his receiver coach and weight trainer, cover my expenses, and also to have a little fun. When we were through, I felt I had the skill and resolve needed for the next level.

The next season I made the 53-man roster.

PERSEVERANCE ROLE MODEL

No one in my life has demonstrated more resolve and will than my brother, Chris. He played basketball at an elite level despite blowing out his anterior cruciate ligament (ACL) in the same leg three times between the ages of ten and sixteen.

For most athletes, a single ACL injury can spell the end of a career, and at the very least, it can mean a year of surgery and recovery. Many who come back from the injury are never the same player they were before the injury.

I'll let Chris tell his own story.

THESE TRIALS MADE ME BETTER

Chris Fowler, graduate assistant, Michigan State University men's basketball

I tore my anterior cruciate ligament the first time when I was ten. I was playing high level-A basketball when I injured it. Ten-year-olds don't know what an ACL is, so I didn't overthink the injury. Initially, my parents weren't able to find a doctor comfortable with, or even willing to, reconstruct my ACL; I was only ten and my growth plates were wide open. Several orthopedists told me to take up the piano or swimming. Eventually, I had the first surgery and did what the doctors and physical therapists told me to do to manage the pain and to get back on the court as soon as possible.

I tore my ACL again five years later while playing high school basketball. I was about to make varsity as a freshman, but my knee became unstable as I grew, and the original graft weakened. I had planned to play half the season on the weakened knee and then have a second ACL surgery. Still, I tweaked the knee during a preseason tournament and had to have surgery right away.

I was too young to worry about college scholarships. All I wanted was to get back and play ball with my friends. It hurt to watch them play and succeed and not be part of it.

Unfortunately, the second surgery was not successful. My body rejected the cadaver ACL they'd grafted into my knee. For the next two years, I unknowingly played ball without a functioning ACL in my right knee.

I still competed at a high level. Some top Division I schools—the University of Cincinnati, Stanford, the University of Dayton, Michigan, and Michigan State—recruited me. But by the middle of my junior year, the knee became unstable again, and many schools backed away. They wouldn't offer me a scholarship if my knee wasn't up to the task. So, I had a third surgery.

Unfortunately, while recovering from that latest ACL surgery, doctors discovered an issue with my kneecap. That required more surgery. For the first time, I fell into a little bit of depression. I thought about quitting

Thankfully, I had a lot of people in my corner.

I told my friend Lee Bailey, a guy I'd played basketball with since we were seven, what I was thinking.

"I don't think I want to do this anymore," I told him. "As soon as I'm able to walk and move again, that's it. I'm done."

Lee wouldn't hear it.

"No, you're not," he said. "We've been through too much. We've come too far for you to quit before we've had a chance to play our last game together."

My dad also convinced me not to quit. In the end, I recovered from the surgery and enrolled at the IMG Academy in Florida. From there, I ended up at Central Michigan University and had a great career. I set a few records. I played professionally for a couple years before my knee told me I was finally done as a player.

As much as I would have loved to play in the NBA, I wouldn't go back and change a thing. Every lesson I learned from those surgeries, pain, and rehab prepared me for where I am today, working as a graduate assistant with the Michigan State men's basketball team. I'm a better coach and mentor because I've been through these trials. Lots of players could play professional basketball here or overseas and come back to coach and mentor players. They could pass on all sorts of advice.

But what could they say to the player facing a catastrophic injury? How many of them can say, "I became a professional in basketball after seven knee surgeries"?

It gives me a certain sense of credibility. If I tell someone how to fight through adversity, they have to believe me. I did it. Even more, I can tell them how to do it better than I did, especially if they reach a certain point in their rehab that I was never able to achieve.

Perseverance is essential for everyone, not just athletes.

Let's say you're a young woman who recently graduated from college. You're struggling to find that first job. Maybe you're feeling like giving up and getting a job bagging groceries or something.

That may be precisely where you need to be at that moment.

Maybe you should bag groceries for now, but you should not give up your bigger dream. What you learn through this experience will serve some greater seen or unseen purpose. The better position will come when the time is right. Meanwhile, you must keep working toward your goal while serving others. If you feel you're being saved for the right time, the right job, and not just any job, then the right one is going to come.

For example, if I could go back and choose, knowing what I know now, I would still want to play at Central Michigan rather than Michigan State because of what I know now. When I was sixteen or seventeen, you couldn't have convinced me to go to CMU over Michigan State. It is said, and in my case, it's true: with age comes wisdom. I'll add to that adversity confronts choices and wisdom informs purpose. God gave me what I needed, not necessarily what I wanted.

One reason people fail to persevere is that they can't appreciate the journey. We strive for goals, and we want to reach those goals now, right this minute. Then, when we reach that goal, we immediately look toward the next goal without appreciating our success. If we reach our goals too fast, the journey is not as sweet.

It's like food. Those things you have to slow cook usually taste better.

Success and perseverance come down to having the heart to serve others. That's how we find the best for ourselves. There's a story in the Bible where Abraham sends his servant to find a wife for his son Isaac. The servant prays to God, "Lord, make me successful today." It's one of the few times the word or concept "success" appears in the Bible. Through the story, God shows us that true success is in how we serve others, not simply in what we do for ourselves.

We usually judge success in others through outward appearances. We look at the kind of car they drive or their profession, or how much money they make, or how many followers they have on social media. That's what success looks like on the surface level.

Real success is helping someone else get where they want to be. Whether you had a successful day or not is not dependent on what you did; it's dependent on what you did to help someone else.

That's one of the things I love about coaching. When I was a player and striving to play in the NBA, everything I did was for myself, and that's one reason I think I didn't get there. In coaching, I know I'm going to get what I need because I'm working so hard to help others realize their dreams.

My greater success is in the making. That's a story yet to be written, but I'm excited to see where it takes me because I'm excited for all the people and players I'll be able to help along the way, knowing what I now know.

Now you can see why Chris is my hero. He is the definition of commitment. He never quit, despite all that adversity he experienced. His work ethic and the process he used to get through tough times helped me develop my own process and mindset. I watched how he handled himself, and I learned. At age ten, Chris certainly could not appreciate how much a torn ACL was going to help him to achieve his success. The same was true of me; who knew a dropped pass, and being cut, would someday lead to authorship?

BORN OR LEARNED?

Perseverance is not a natural talent. It's not like height or speed or vertical leap, things that are mostly the product of the genetic lottery (although any trait can be improved with practice). It's a skill that can be learned and honed over time.

The first question to ask yourself is: How serious am I about this goal or dream? Everyone can endure, but how you persevere comes down to your degree of want. Your discipline. Achieving anything of worth is difficult, so let's explore the role discipline plays in that process.

CHAPTER THREE

DISCIPLINE

"Discipline is the difference between what you want now and what you want most."

AUTHOR UNKNOWN

"The only discipline that lasts is self-discipline."

BUM PHILLIPS

Ask any eight-year-old soccer player or Pee Wee football player what discipline is, and they'll all be able to rattle off exactly what we've all been told by coaches and teachers. They'll tell you it means getting up every day and working hard and not complaining. That's all true when it comes to the large concept of discipline. But what is discipline in practice? What does it look like every day? And what is the effect of discipline on a person's life as a whole?

I have been blessed with people who held me accountable and ensured I maintained the work ethic necessary to excel. It began with my parents, who instilled in me a work ethic that has carried me from youth to the pros. I can remember my mother buying me a weight vest and pants and insisting that I begin the day working out while wearing them. I remember my father's dedication to going to work every day.

It paid off when I got to Denver. When you're around a guy like Peyton, his sense of discipline is contagious. Whether it was on the practice field or in meetings, I was never as diligent as I was during the time I played with him.

That's the thing about discipline—you have to work hard to maintain it.

When Peyton retired, I let my self-regulation and concentration lapse. I worked hard for the quarterbacks who succeeded him, but I didn't work as hard as I could have. Getting cut in Denver should have awakened me, but it didn't. I landed with the Chicago Bears and eventually got cut.

From there, I got another chance to play with one of the game's greats—Tom Brady of the New England Patriots. My stay in New England was brief, but being around an implacable player like Brady reminded me of what got me into the league in the first place.

Discipline.

Doing the right thing, even (especially) when no one is watching.

NEVER LETTING ANYTHING GO TO WASTE

When I was a kid, Saturday mornings were not for sleeping in. They were for rising early, cooking breakfast, and getting chores done. These routines were meant to show us what it meant to be a man, helping us accumulate the little bits of knowledge that would lead to fulfilled adult lives.

My father was our basketball and baseball coach for years, and he started every practice with conditioning. We'd rather scrimmage and compete, but he'd make us get in shape before we could get down to the fun. The drills and conditioning built our tenacity and work habits.

He held us accountable. He had penalties for being late. When he coached basketball, he insisted the team arrive at the gym two hours before the game.

He understood that self-control, preparation, and a strict

regimen pave the way to success—not just in sports but in life as well. He emphasized the mental, physical, and spiritual aspects of a successful life. The mental part meant staying focused. The physical element involved the training regimen. The spiritual element had three components: belief in yourself, belief in your team, and belief in the culture that helps you prepare. He talked a lot when I was growing up about the importance of having a spiritual foundation in your life.

I'm sure my dad had aspirations to be a professional athlete. He was a great athlete, having played both basketball and baseball in college, but he also knew that few people make it to the pros. Consequently, he emphasized building a foundation in education. He believed a prosperous and healthy life required education and that education commanded the same persistence and routine as sports: you need to put in the work if you want to get results.

He refused to allow anything to go to waste, especially talent. If a player showed that they had some skill at a particular game, my father would do whatever he could to ensure that ability was put to use. Discipline—doing the little things right all the time—was the foundation for everything else he taught us.

My parents taught us to respect ourselves and those around us. We primarily played team sports, and my father stressed that on teams, you must know your role and do your job. Everyone on the team. When that happens, you're more likely to be successful.

The youth organization that my dad helped form and that we were a part of was very challenging. We focused on more than playing. We learned how to eat right, how to practice with purpose, and how to absorb what we learned in practice. The coaches set strict rules about how we dressed and our appearance. No earrings, for instance. Hair combed. Pants pulled up to our waist and not hanging low over our butts. We had to be on time. They taught us about public speaking, even: after practice, we had to get up and address the group and discuss what we'd learned that day in practice.

Through this, we learned how to handle both success and disappointment. We learned to be humble when we won and respectful when we lost.

PROS NEED IT TOO

Other than natural ability, discipline is the single most important dish that you must bring to the table. This holds true in all facets of life.

Often, discipline is one of the few things you can control. No one else has a say in whether you're deliberate or purposeful in your work and practice. Some might say, well, you can control effort, and I totally agree, EXCEPT to me, effort and discipline are the same things.

Determined and focused individuals know how to limit distractions. They zero in on the essentials of whatever they're doing. I've seen good players make it to the top, and I've seen gifted players not make it at all. Most often, it's the ability to concentrate and to ignore distractions that make the difference.

It's rarely a question of talent. The NFL and NBA don't turn away players because they're too talented. But talented players who lack discipline? That's another story. People who don't have enough self-control and persistence fall short of their dreams and goals.

Professional players shouldn't expect a team or business to invest millions of dollars in them if they aren't disciplined. It's no different for any employer. Resources are finite. Hiring and training people is expensive. So why would anyone invest in you if you don't have the maturity, determination, and a sense of purpose to get the job done and help the company meet its goals? In professional sports, there is an additional pitfall of leisure time. Teams want to know that their players won't do anything during their downtime that will affect the team's investment.

I saw the effects of a focused regimen on a team's culture when I arrived at Michigan State. Self-control becomes a big issue in college. Suddenly, a few dozen of us were on our own for the first time in our lives. It didn't take long to see who was going to put in the work and who would not, who was going to devote the extra time and who was just going to do the bare minimum to get by.

BEGIN WITH ONE LITTLE THING EVERY DAY

Discipline is a daily task. Every day I do something that makes me a better player.

Every.

Day.

It may not be something physical, like a session with my footwork coach or in the weight room. It might be prayer, visualization, extra catching drills, or going into the team building on a day off. Other times, I'll be working in my journal, taking an Epsom salt bath, or meditating.

There's no one specific thing that I do, but I always do something, every day, to bring me closer to achieving my dreams and goals.

It's an effective strategy. Anyone—not just professional

athletes—benefits from a regular, well-defined regimen. Dedicating time every day to one thing that's going to help you get where you want to be sounds like a small thing, but it's the foundation of discipline.

Religion is a crucial part of my own approach. Cornerback Aqib Talib once explained his philosophy on prayer to me this way: "Pray like everything depends on God, and work like everything depends on you. When I come to work, you never have to ask me if I know my assignment or if I'm ready to play. And I pray just as hard."

DISCIPLINE IS PUT TO THE TEST EVERY DAY

Discipline is that moment when the gravity of your butt is outweighed by the gravity of your brain. Long-term success is accomplished over thousands of small moments when your mind forces you to keep going, no matter how much you may not want to. The disciplined mind stays in control and forces the body to take that next step, study that next chapter, or show up to that early practice. Discipline is your brain believing it is bigger than any obstacle. It is the mental awareness and presence of space that when your brain says, "Be early," your body can only comply. No matter how lazy or tired your body might feel, your butt will never weigh more than the gravity of your brain pushing you forward. In a phrase, "It's mind over matter when it matters most."

When I was getting ready for the NFL Combine, I lived like a monk. The Combine is a weeklong evaluation held each February at the Lucas Oil Stadium in Indianapolis, where college players hoping to be chosen during the draft two months later are put through a standardized set of physical tests.

How you perform on those tests can determine not only whether you get drafted but how high in the draft you are selected. The higher you're taken, the bigger the contract offered. The Combine has a real-world financial impact on your life.

The stakes are high.

To prepare, a few of my friends and fellow competitors went to Tampa to train for several weeks. At night, some of them would go out on the town. Nothing crazy, but they stayed out late sometimes, ate things that definitely were not on the training table, and didn't get the sleep they needed.

I was determined to do things differently. I stayed in my room between sessions. I ate only the food provided by the training site. I never went out drinking, and I made sure I got all the massages and post-training medical treatments recommended to me.

We spent three months in Tampa, and my monastic life

paid off. I performed well at the Combine. I controlled what was within my control.

My detailed approach to training and preparation continues to be tested every day. It would be easy to relax and stop doing the million little things that keep you at the highest level of the sport, but those kinds of lapses have hurt me in the past, so I avoid them.

Money, of course, can be a distraction for players. My first year in the league was the first time I'd regularly gotten a whole bunch of money. Lump sums of it, every week. Factor in the loose schedule and wide swaths of free time, and you can find yourself on a slippery slope, discipline-wise. Money, football, freedom. School's over and you get to play football every day.

But the money and freedom come with heavy responsibility. You must do everything right to play at the highest level.

Whatever your line of work, you've got to come ready every day. If you find a way to be at your best every moment of every day, you'll discover that discipline is at the core of it all.

Discipline gets you up out of bed early, when it would be so much easier to dig deeper into those covers.

It's the thing that gets me to every meeting early, even if the last thing I feel like doing that day is sitting in a conference room.

Discipline is the fuel that keeps the sports car moving forward and always ready to perform.

LIVING WITH SUCCESS

Discipline will lead to some level of success, no matter what goal you're seeking or dream you're pursuing. Discipline is like a supervisor.

It will lead you to where you want to go.

It can help you stay there once you've arrived.

But does it help you handle success? As we'll see in the next chapter, sometimes your biggest problems show up after you've become successful.

CHAPTER FOUR

HANDLING SUCCESS

"If you study the happiest, healthiest, most satisfied people of our world, you will see that each and every one of them has found their passion in life and then spent their days pursuing it...Once you are concentrating your mental power and energy on a pursuit that you love, abundance flows into your life, and all your desires are fulfilled with ease and grace."

ROBIN SHARMA, *THE MONK WHO SOLD HIS FERRARI*

Most professional athletes will tell you that reaching their goals took a profound level of concentration and hard work. There were hours on the practice fields, hundreds of thousands of reps in the weight room, wind sprints in the midday heat, and late nights in the film room studying your opponents and studying yourself.

The pros I admire continue that level of commitment

after they've made the roster, signed the contract, or earned the starting job. In fact, that need to evolve—as a player but also as a person—never ends.

Success is a beautiful thing, and I'm not saying you shouldn't allow yourself to enjoy it. You should. Buy your mom a new house, like my friend Draymond Green did. Take private jets to vacation destinations, if that's your thing. Hire a chef. You've worked hard to earn your success, so enjoy the benefits.

Keep in mind, though, that success—and how you respond to it—is going to reveal to the world who you really are. Just as times of adversity can be a measure of our character, so can times of prosperity. Despite your fame and achievements, do you continue to live with humility?

Do you continue to nurture your mind and body?

Do you strive to live a life of purpose and help others?

Do you have the courage to continue to challenge yourself?

Do you continue in the journey?

Success carries its own levels of stress. Watch Bill Belichick on the sidelines after the Patriots have scored a touchdown. Belichick is one of the most successful head football coaches of the modern era. Still, he does not celebrate after a touchdown. Some coaches are pumping their fists or dancing down the sideline, but Belichick is more likely to pull out his notes and start writing something down. He looks worried, even when the Patriots are extending a lead.

Why is that?

"I'm happy when we score," he explained after a 2017 game against Miami that New England won 43–0. "But there's a decision that has to be made on the next play and the play after that and then the next series....A big part of my job is planning ahead for the next situation."

That explains a lot. People like Belichick do not let success go to their heads. They are not content with the status quo. In their minds, there is always something more you can achieve, something more you can do to get better.

BACK TO HIGH SCHOOL

In high school, I was more passionate about basketball than I was about football. Every year my team was in the mix for the state championship.

The composition of the team in my sophomore year was a

great bunch of guys, but on paper, we weren't as talented as some of the other teams in the state. But we had an edge because we ignored what was *supposed* to happen and focused solely on the games—on what we *could* do, even if we were the only ones who saw it.

What happened?

State champions! That's right!

The teams in my junior and senior years were even deeper and had more-talented players than our previous squad. In my senior year, we weren't just the best team in Michigan—we were ranked fourth in the *nation*, ahead of perennial powerhouse Oak Hill Academy. People expected great things from us. We were taller. Faster. More athletic.

And we knew it.

But other teams came ready for us. They'd heard the hype, but it didn't seem to affect them. We believed the hype, and it did affect us. Every team we played that year came in laser-focused and well-prepared. They'd had their games with us circled on the calendar for months, and I'm sure some of them had trained and practiced all year with the idea of beating us.

As a result, we ran into teams that worked harder than us—who prepared better than we did. Never mind the national rankings—we didn't even win the state championship in either of those years.

Finding success is one thing, but it is only *half* the thing. The other half, the more critical part, is learning how to handle that success.

We didn't, and we paid for it.

LOOKING AHEAD

Although I try not to be distracted by the past or the future, I also believe that the best way to handle success is to think about what's next. What's your role in the next play? What's your plan for next year? What are you going to do when your career is over?

One of the most vital things I learned about handling success came after we won the Super Bowl in 2015 with Denver. Suddenly all these opportunities are flying at you. People want you to join this or appear in that. Old friends suddenly want to hang out. You find yourself saying yes to a lot of these opportunities and relationships that seem like they will help with life after football. I quickly realized that the best thing I could do was this:

Remember what got you to where you are.

Don't forget the attitude, practice, and diligence that brought you success because you still need them and will continue to need them. What got you there is what is going to keep you there.

Here are some tips on how to behave after you have experienced success.

SAVOR YOUR TIME

In the book *The Monk Who Sold His Ferrari*, author Robin Sharma writes how "Time slips through our hands like grains of sand, never to return again." No one understands how quickly their circumstances can change like a professional football player. The game is brutal, and careers can end in an instant. The key is not to fear losing all you've worked for but to savor each moment.

This advice works for anyone—not just pro athletes. It's OK to guard your time and to have the courage to say no sometimes.

IT'S NOT WHAT YOU EARN BUT WHAT YOU DO WITH WHAT YOU EARN

I learned this from Draymond. When I talked to him

about his views on handling success and keeping things in perspective, he said it boiled down to what was important to you.

"For some people, it's fame that's most important to them," he said. "For some people, it's money. They emphasize these things, and it gets to their head.

"I have fame and money, but neither of those things matters to me. It's what you do with that fame and that money that counts. Fame and money should be there only as resources to the end goal, which is to help improve the lives of others."

This should give you an idea of why I love Draymond Green. After signing a new contract with the Golden State Warriors, he donated $3.1 million to Michigan State. He's also part of an investment fund for promoting entrepreneurship in Flint, Michigan.

"I don't get off on me, me, me," he said. "Fame and wealth...it can't be all about you. If it is, it's all for nothing. It has to be about helping people."

I'm sure, by now, you can see there is a common thread in the people I love and surround myself with: they all seek to use their journey to improve someone else's journey.

My support system includes my family and friends. I think one reason I'm in the league is that I grew up with so many people who were talented and shared the same dream. I've had a lot of friends who've experienced NFL games or NBA games, so they know what it's like, and we can talk about the challenges and the successes.

Success can break relationships, or it can enhance them. It's only enhanced my friendships. My friends from high school and college are still my closest friends. My college roommate came out for the Super Bowl in 2015. My whole family was there. Draymond was there.

This is your family.

They go as you go.

They'll feel your highs, and they'll feel your lows too. Because they are a constant, they continue to help me to find the balance.

When you're losing or something has happened in your career, your family will be there for you. They often can't relate to what's happening to you, so they ask, "Are you OK?" and you answer, "Yeah. Life is just happening to me, just like it happens to you." They may not know what to say to you, but that's OK because they will always be there to listen.

LOOK FOR LITTLE VICTORIES

We all hit rough patches in our lives, times when nothing seems to be going right. When the success you've experienced seems to be avoiding you. Get back into the habit of being successful by celebrating little victories. Focus on the things that are going right, and before you know it, more things are going to start going your way. As a good friend of mine told me once, "Success comes in being great in short spans of time, not all the time."

Little victories add up to big ones.

STUDY HOW OTHERS HANDLE THEIR SUCCESS

I admire athletes who've had long-term success in a sport where short-term is the norm. I watch how they handle themselves, even as the spotlight in which they play and live threatens to rob them of everything they've achieved. Not only do these people survive their success, but they have also mastered it.

You have to handle the good times as well as the bad. The good times can be a trap. If you find too much comfort from the last few plays that went well, your hunger and determination can ebb. You might think you can take a break.

Comfort is the enemy.

My former teammate at Michigan State, Darqueze Dennard, is an excellent example of someone who avoids complacency like it's the plague. Darqueze plays cornerback for the Cincinnati Bengals, who drafted him in the first round after he won both the Jack Tatum Trophy and the Jim Thorpe Award as the best defensive back in college football. Darqueze grew up in Dry Branch, Georgia, a small town in the south-central part of the state with a population of just over three thousand people.

"You definitely can't get complacent," he said. "Once you get complacent, you might as well hang it up because there's some kid out there who's seventeen or eighteen right now who is busting their butt to come and take your spot. Every year they are trying to get somebody better than you. That means you have to get better every year."

Playing cornerback is possibly the toughest job in football. Cornerbacks cover the fastest person on the field—the wide receiver. The receiver knows where he is going and pulls out every trick they have to leave their defender in the dust. Even when someone like Darqueze can stay with a receiver, they have to contend with quarterbacks like Tom Brady and Drew Brees, who can thread a needle with a pass.

Darqueze has succeeded for three reasons: he's competitive, he's disciplined, and he's willing to make sacrifices to get better. His attitude infuses his entire life. He doesn't drink because he knows that might give him an advantage over an opponent who stayed out late. He studies film like a madman so he can find patterns in receivers' habits and tendencies.

"You have to take chances," he told me once, "but they have to be educated. It's got to be something you've noticed before. If you're wrong, you're wrong. But if you've done your homework, you have nothing to be ashamed of."

I admire Darqueze because he's consistent and always trying to get better. He trains diligently in the off-season, and he'll try new and different methods to make himself better mentally or physically. He doesn't watch football unless he's studying film, and in his spare time, he reads.

"I'm into learning new things," he told me recently. "Reading is an escape for me, but it also teaches me new things."

THE PITFALLS OF SUCCESS

Some of you reading this might be wondering: How hard can it be to handle success? You work hard, and you win. What's not to love about that? Why not enjoy it?

The point is that success presents its own challenges. If you're someone who is always striving to get better—and I hope by picking up this book that you are that kind of person—then success poses an important question:

What's next?

If you're an entrepreneur and you've just taken your company from a $100,000-a-year organization working out of a garage to a $10-million company with dozens of employees, what's next for you? Are you going to rest on your success or look for even more? Now that you're a CEO and not another small business owner, does that mean you don't need to keep learning and training yourself?

No. Of course not. You're going to keep growing. But you face an even bigger task because growing a $10-million company is more challenging that expanding a mom-and-pop outfit.

But that's just one of the reasons why we all need to learn to handle success. Here are some others.

Right after we won the Super Bowl when I was in Denver, Peyton retired. No one on the team seemed concerned at first. Even though we'd lost a great QB, everyone knew we still had a great team; indeed, we had not lost our great and imposing defensive line. The thing is, though, once you win the Super Bowl, everyone is gunning for you. At times, it seems that even your family, your friends, and your fans are among those gunning for you; after all, they too have tasted sweet victory, and enjoyed it, and they want it again immediately. The game against your team instantly becomes the biggest game on every other team's schedule. You're trying to repeat. Still, the expectations around winning a Super Bowl are so high that they raise everyone else's competition level against you. That's why back-to-back Super Bowl wins are so rare. In the end, we weren't able to repeat either.

Earlier, I talked about the exultation of winning the Super Bowl, the satisfaction of a moment achieved through a lifetime of work. Achieving that lifetime of work again in a short twelve months was near impossible because the journey now was starting from a different level. Although the tenets of success—resolve, patience, discipline, and perseverance—remained the same on balance, effectively installing them again was difficult. The appreciation for them was most assuredly lacking, given that the focus was now on the prize alone.

So, for the new CEO of the $10-million business, trust what got you there—redoubling your principles may not grow you to $20 million in the very next year, but it will grow you for many years to come. Your daily grind and routine got you here; your daily grind and routine will get you there.

MANAGING TIME

Time is a commodity, a resource like any other finite and perishable material. You need to guard it and ensure that you're using it to your advantage. You can't get where you want to go on someone else's itinerary. Set your own. Protect your time.

This is where that discipline we talked about in the last chapter comes into play. Doing the right things every day, beginning with the small things. When you waste time on the things that don't make you better, when you fail to rest and pause and refresh, you lose your joy and opportunity for the pursuit.

Remember to spend time improving yourself as a human being. Learning is a great passion of mine. When I'm not working on my game, I'm working on learning how to live an amazing life, how to impact other peoples' lives, and how to better spend my time here on Earth while I have it.

An undrafted free agent on the practice squad makes approximately ten percent of the minimum NFL salary. It's not bad money for a twenty-two-year-old with no debt, but it's also not wealth. I was in the NFL and surrounded by a lot of very wealthy, very young men. What they had and what they were able to do was also available to me on a much, much smaller scale, and while the immature me said, "Go for it!" the me with the degree in economics said, "Go for your future!" I have one hard-learned lesson in finance: Invest in you first.

When my father graduated from Central State University in 1978 with a degree in business operations, his first job paid him a whopping $18,000 a year. This was the equivalent of one-tenth what a plant manager in the auto industry was making in their first year. Five years later, my father used his savings and invested in himself. He went to graduate school, obtained a master's degree, and went on to surpass his initial goal of being a plant manager and eventually ascended to the level of Executive Vice President at Ford Motor Company. Although his salary continued to increase exponentially in those first five years after he graduated college, he knew bigger increases required even bigger sacrifice.

I had minimal savings from my practice squad salary after my first year. Of course, like everyone, I had to pay rent, eat, drive, and live. Initially, I was hesitant to take Julius Thomas up on his offer to join him in Los Angeles to train in the off-season. LA is not only expensive, it's alluring—*Lifestyles of the Rich and Famous* all day, every day. I could easily have returned home to Michigan, worked out at Michigan State, and kept the few dollars I had managed to hold on to.

But my goal was to start for the Denver Broncos the next season. I was all-in. I used every dime of my savings, believing in the promise that I had made to myself. Holding on to a small savings is wise, but if that small amount is the difference between peace of mind that you've pursued the greatness within you, or choosing the comfort of "at least"—buy peace! Don't be afraid to start over. If at first you don't succeed, try, try again.

The decision my dad made to get a master's degree and the decision I made to move to LA for a summer to train were respectively uncomfortable. My brother Chris always says, "Getting to the top often employs you to be comfortable with being uncomfortable." My mom says, "Work before you play, and all your life you will thrive."

As you know from the first chapter of this book, I made the team my second year in the league, and I even started some games. Oh, and by the way, that year I became a Super Bowl champion.

You may be working at your first job, second job, or third job. You may have quit your job or career to start and restart your business. Don't be afraid to enjoy life from the cheap seats while you're forging ahead. I will reiterate: the prize is in the journey.

Now let me put my economics degree to work for you: in life and in business, there will be trade-offs. To get one thing, we must give up another thing. You have the freedom to choose the timing of the trade-off, and that's when the opportunity cost is measured. For me, it was simple. The average career of an NFL player is five years. The average career of an undrafted player is two years. I had no time to waste; I had to invest in my training immediately.

On the other hand, for my father, at age twenty-two coming out of college, he had time to observe the experiences and career development of corporate professionals in the manufacturing and auto industries. After five years, his career was more ripe for advancement with a master's degree, and so he made the move.

There must be an incentive to make the trade-off at the time that you make it. The incentive can, and most definitely should, involve money and a better quality of life, but incentive should be measured by your "want to." In other words, trade up to your calling, and it will be your life's good work.

Success can make you blind to the methods you used to succeed. A grateful heart and soul will go a long way toward avoiding this trap, but anyone can easily fall into it. The journey feels complete when the goal arrives, even though, in reality, it's only just begun.

When my playing days are over, I see myself working with other NFL athletes and young entrepreneurs as a process engagement mentor. I want to help new players handle their success. These players need help managing their money, handling the pressure, building relationships, and dealing with the day-to-day stresses of life. I've seen examples of athletes who handle success adeptly, and I've seen others who don't.

The next several segments of this book are very personal, and very football-focused. I'll discuss my exposure to different training techniques, coaching styles, process strategies, and philosophical developments to become a better professional athlete. However, each of these modalities mattered in my writing of this book, and each can, and should, be used by you in whatever you do because all skills are transferable. High-level skills transfer into high-level results.

A big piece of my advice will be about developing the right mindset. In the next chapter, I'll talk about how to do that.

————

CHAPTER FIVE

MINDSET

"[T]he belief that cherished qualities can be developed creates a passion for learning...The passion for stretching yourself and sticking to it, even (or especially) when it's not going well, is the hallmark of the growth mindset. This is the mindset that allows people to thrive during some of the most challenging times in their lives."

DR. CAROL DWECK, *MINDSET: THE NEW PSYCHOLOGY OF SUCCESS*

In 2015, the year we went to Super Bowl 50, I didn't play offense for the first two games of the regular season. This was my first year off the practice squad, and I'd had a good preseason. I'd caught ten passes, and I'd led the team in receiving yards in one game with sixty-seven, and I'd scored in our last preseason game against the Cardinals. Still, I didn't get into our first two games against the Baltimore Ravens and the Kansas City Chiefs.

In week three, we traveled to Detroit to face the Lions, and I was itching to get into the game. This was a hometown crowd for me, and I was eager to show everyone what I could do. The coaches decided who played, so that was out of my hands. So, I concentrated on the things I *could* control.

I'd been working on my mental preparation since my season on the practice squad. When I got cut that first year, I knew I had to work harder—not just on my physical talent but also on my psychological skills and awareness.

Being around NFL players every day, I learned that the best players had the strongest minds.

Everyone in the NFL is a great athlete. Everyone is highly skilled. They all have remarkable gifts of speed, strength, and coordination. The primary thing that separates the great ones from the good ones is mental resilience. They can remain calm when a hundred thousand people are screaming at them at the top of their lungs.

The best players are those who are focused, calm, and persistent. They train and practice with great intensity, but they bring that same discipline to their mental training. They control their emotions. They actively drive away any thoughts of self-doubt. They visualize their success.

I learned some of these practices watching interviews with Michael Jordan and Kobe Bryant. You always hear people talking about those players' mindsets. They have that killer instinct. Strength of will. It helped me to learn how they developed their attitudes and approaches to the game. I also read what Phil Jackson had to say about the power of meditation and mindfulness. I read a book called *The Mindful Athlete* by George Mumford, who also worked with the Lakers and Bulls when Bryant and Jordan played on those teams.

I have also spent time with Dr. Rick Perea, a sports psychologist who worked with the Broncos. Many teams make sports psychologists available to players, and Dr. P is one of the best. He's helped so many people. When he worked for the Nuggets in the NBA, he helped one player improve his free-throw shooting by merely changing the way the player took a deep breath at the foul line.

MINDSET AND MOTIVATION

When he talks about motivation, Rick Perea draws a comparison between process and outcome.

People who focus on outcomes have **extrinsic motivation**. They've got to be All-Pro. They've got to get that new contract or that deal with Adidas. They've got to make so many catches in the next game. Many people, including many professional athletes, are too focused on extrinsic motivation.

Intrinsic motivation is where you focus on the process you need to achieve the desired outcome. Process is about technique and mastering the things that you can control. Like footwork. Knowing your routes. Throwing a good block. Intrinsic motivation is about being the best you can be today with what you can control.

Rick explained the science and psychology behind this to me. When you focus on process and the things you can control, your anxiety goes down. When your anxiety goes down, you're on the parasympathetic side of your autonomic nervous system. When you're on the parasympathetic side, your heart rate goes down, breathing is relaxed, muscle tension decreases, and your thinking is clarified.

You perform better.

When you're on the sympathetic side of things, your breathing is more rapid and shallow, your heart rate is elevated, and your muscles tense up. It's like, Oh shit.

What am I going to do? It doesn't matter who you are or what you do for a living: when you're on the sympathetic side, performance declines.

Dr. P isn't telling us not to have goals. Of course, you should have goals.

State them.

Write them down.

Put them out there.

Then put them away in a shoebox and focus every day on the process that will help you reach them.

With the Broncos, I played with Demaryius Thomas and Emmanuel Sanders. These guys were both big-name receivers and pro bowlers. They cast a deep shadow. But that didn't matter to me when I focused on the process and not the outcome. I couldn't control how other receivers played, but I could undoubtedly manage my training, practice, and preparation. When I focused on that, I was relaxed and ready. I may have been the designated third or fourth receiver on the team, but when the ball came my way, I was number one, and the expectations were the same. Mind preparedness for any moment can propel your career.

The University of Alabama is, and has been, one of the most successful football programs of all time. They've been a threat to win the national championship every year for the last decade or more. But when you visit the University of Alabama football facility and read the inspirational messages on the wall, you don't see anything about winning.

Nothing.

Instead, there are signs like "Love the process" and "Be the process" and "Trust the process." When you understand that you live in the process every day, then your outcome will come to you instead of you having to search it out. Success will come to you.

Here's another important thing I learned from Dr. P: winning is a *symptom* of process. In the NFL, teams like the New England Patriots win so much because they have the right climate and the right culture. It's not their Xs and Os. It's what they do every day to improve their chances of winning.

Dr. P compares it to selling real estate. If a real estate agent has to sell twenty homes a month, they shouldn't obsess about that quota. They should focus on all the little things that will bring around those twenty sales— communication skills, open houses, email marketing. If the agent focuses on the things they can control, they'll end up with those twenty sales.

IMPROVING YOUR MINDSET

Dr. P gave me a big bag of tricks for building and honing my mindset. For instance, I learned about the power of affirmations—simple statements that motivate you and inspire you to do better. Affirmations keep you focused on your goals and can actually change the way you think and behave.

Dr. P helped me develop these positive affirmations, and I go through them every morning. He also taught me how to visualize and picture the success I wanted. You see yourself making the big play, or you envision what you will do for each play.

You use these tools to develop a frame of mind where self-doubt is diminished.

After that first year on the practice squad, I wasn't sure if I should go home to train for the upcoming season or move to LA and train there. Going to LA was a risk. I would be spending my savings to chase this dream of a career in the NFL with no guarantee that it would pay off, and I had no other employment prospects in tow.

My mind was playing tricks on me, so I overcame that with some tricks of my own. I asked myself:

Do I want to do this or don't I?

BE THE CHANGE YOU WANT TO SEE

My mom likes the picture of Moses Wright from the trial of Roy Bryant and J.W. Milam for the murder of Emmett Till. Moses Wright was a small man, measuring about five foot three. In 1955, Mr. Wright, a sharecropper in the cotton-growing segregated Mississippi Delta, invited his fourteen-year-old great-nephew Emmett to visit for the summer. The rest of the story is very well known.

Mr. Wright was a prosecution witness and when asked if he recognized the men who murdered his nephew, against all odds and the almost certainty of his own death and possibly the deaths of members of his family, Mr. Wright stood up in the witness box and pointed directly at the defendants.

I'm sure Mr. Wright wondered to himself, if not aloud, whether he should take the risk of his honest testimony; indeed, before the trial, he had put his wife on a train to Chicago fearing for her life. She begged him not to testify. Given the time in this country's history, it is likely that his fellow sharecroppers would have fully understood his decision to avoid the trial altogether. The risk was just too great.

Something about the mental fortitude of Mr. Wright reminds my mom of "do your job." I can imagine him saying, "I want to be the change I want to see."

If you want to do this, then do everything you can to succeed.

Go to LA and train.

You never want to fail because you were afraid to try something risky. The road to success is not always the safest route. You have a tiny window of opportunity in the NFL.

Careers are short. Contracts, in any situation, aren't guaranteed.

If you want to squeeze your leg through that window, you have to blow it up with your mind.

GETTING THE CALL IN GAME THREE

I prepared for the Detroit game the way I always do.

The Broncos, like most teams in the NFL, scripted the first fifteen plays on offense. I had set aside time to envision each play. I pictured my routes. I visualized the blocks I would make. I imagined catching any ball thrown to me.

Most football fans focus on where the ball is going, whether it's a pass or running play. The rest just seems random and chaotic. It isn't.

Every player on the field has a precise role to play and after each game, each player receives a report on how well they handled their assignment. Did they run the right route? Did they block the safety? Did they run their route deep enough to take the cornerback out of the play? Leading up to Detroit, I carefully visualized all these things so I would be ready if I got into the game.

I got into the Detroit game for our third offensive drive. The coaches were letting me show what I could do.

Although Peyton was throwing primarily to Demaryius Thomas, Emmanuel Sanders, and Owen Daniels in that game, I was targeted four times. I caught all four passes, gaining fifty yards total. Each catch was a first down.

When I was on the field, I never felt like I was in a high-pressure situation. I wasn't nervous. I felt no anxiety. You'd think that I would have been a basket case, this being my first time playing in the NFL, back in my hometown, with about a hundred of my friends and family in the stands. But I was calm. I felt like I had been there before. I felt like I'd run those plays before and knew precisely what was going to happen. I wasn't thinking about what was going on or how it was going on. I let things happen just as I had visualized them. After the game, I was swept over by a sense of relief and satisfaction.

My mental preparation had worked.

I'd played great. At home. In front of my family. People I knew.

It was awesome.

Dr. P would say that I'd been successful in staying on my parasympathetic side.

"Think of it this way, Bennie," he told me recently. "When you're playing in your backyard or at the park or rec center, you play freely, without fear. It's when you're playing on Sunday in front of a hundred thousand people and the television cameras that the sympathetic system rears its ugly head. The great players can tap into their parasympathetic in those situations. They're free. Trust that and stay in that parasympathetic side of things where thinking is clear and muscles are relaxed. That's where performance lives."

THE MOST IMPORTANT THING

Drake says it in a song:

> "See, the power of the mind is not a joke
>
> Man, I said that I would do it and I did"

Those lyrics speak to me all the time.

Your mindset is what gets you up every morning for your workout. Mindset is what kept me going when I got cut by Chicago and New England. I kept getting up at 6:00 a.m. because I wanted to be ready. I got up when I had no reason (no team, no game) to get up for. Readiness is as much a mental attribute as it is a physical attribute. When an opportunity came, I wanted to be ready.

That mindset paid off when I got picked up by New York. I worked out for them on a Monday and signed with them on Tuesday. I didn't waste time. I made flash-cards, and I learned the playbook in five days. I walked through the plays myself. During the game, I made one catch and had no missed assignments. I had no mental errors.

Mindset is everything. You have to have a healthy mindset because you never know when your opportunity is going to come. If you keep working and grinding every single day, your mind is getting sharper and sharper.

I've been on an NFL roster every year since developing this mindset. But as with physical training, you have to work on your mental preparation continually. I do something new with my brain or mental capacity every year in the off-season.

Last year I worked on mindfulness and meditation. I got up to meditating for forty-five minutes a day. It's a pure high, but it takes practice.

This year I worked on neurofeedback. You have a map drawn of your brain that shows how your neurons are firing. Neurofeedback strengthens, calms, and stabilizes the mind, giving you greater neurological flexibility. You don't get "stuck" in a state of anxiety or anger.

Here's how it works: you are hooked up to a computer, and it allows you to change your brainwaves to create a more focused, happy, relaxed, loving, and productive brain. I did about a hundred sessions during off-season. Neurofeedback helps you get into a flow state where everything feels like it's going just right. You're at peace with yourself, and you are in the moment, not worrying about the past or the future.

There are games that you play or that you learn. You do your breathing, and the brain does its own work. They play sounds or music that the brain likes, but if you're not focused on the moment, the music gets choppy. The mind wants to hear the flow of the music, though, so it adjusts to smooth it out.

I've seen talented people not reach their goals because they didn't have the right mindset when they got their opportunity. You see it all the time. First-round draft picks who fail, and people ask, "What happened? What got into him?" Nothing got into him. His mind simply wasn't ready for the challenge. When highly regarded football players come out of college and fail miserably in the pros, it's rarely due to a lack of physical skills or talent. It's almost always mental.

That's why someone like Tom Brady is going to be around forever. That's why Larry Fitzgerald is so successful. Those guys are mentally strong. Kobe Bryant—mentally tough enough to play for eighteen years. LeBron James. Mentally tough on and off the floor.

PROCESS AND DESIRE: JULIUS THOMAS

When I think of the importance of process, I often think of my former Denver teammate Julius Thomas. Julius is from Stockton, California, a tough city in the Central Valley of California. After several great years in the NFL, Julius retired and went to work on his PhD in psychology. Not many NFL tight ends follow that postcareer path, but Julius isn't like many other NFL players.

"I struggled with every facet of the game except desire," he once told me. "If there's one thing that I would attribute my success to, it would be desire."

Julius started out as a basketball player, a six-foot-four power forward. Despite an injury that nearly ended his playing days when he was sixteen, Julius earned a basketball scholarship to Portland State in the Big Sky Conference and graduated in four years.

Though he could have played professionally in Europe, Julius chose instead to stay at Portland for a fifth year and go out for the football team. He'd always wanted to try football. Still, with his scholarship and focus in high school on basketball, the opportunity never materialized. His basketball coach in college declined his request to play football. But when his basketball eligibility ran out, he showed up in the football coach's office offering to play.

"Well, we aren't in the habit of turning away six-four receivers," the coach said. "Suit up."

Julius struggled initially. He couldn't block. He didn't understand the plays or the jargon. Every day that spring, he was the third- or fourth-string tight end.

Then one day toward the end of practice, one of the coaches said, "Let's see if we can get this guy to catch a pass. Maybe he can do that. He sure as hell can't block."

So, they called a five-yard drag route, one of the easiest plays in football. Julius came off the line, turned to collect the pass, and took off running. Past the linebackers. Past the secondary. He didn't stop until he reached the end zone.

The next day, the same thing.

More of the coaches started watching. They threw him some more balls, and he ran by everybody. Another house call. Then another.

Julius couldn't block or understand the plays, but he could catch the ball and was difficult to tackle.

Suddenly, practice became a little more intense for Julius. If the team was going to be able to use him in games, Julius needed to learn the techniques.

There were footwork drills, O-line drills, blocking drills, running routes. He took breaks with the coaches so he could pick their brains. He scheduled evening and morning sessions with any one of the five quarterbacks willing to throw to him as he ran one route after another, learning the cuts and angles and corners.

He had a lot to learn, but Julius kept on coming.

That spring, Julius called his brother.

"I'm going to be in the NFL next year," he told him.

"Dude, you just started playing three weeks ago."

"All I need is a tryout," Julius said. "I just wanted to tell you the plan."

Then he set about making that plan happen. He told himself to play without fear. He told himself that no one believed in him the way he believed in himself. He learned what it meant to be a football player.

He never stopped coming.

In his one year of college football, he was an all-conference tight end, averaged 17.5 yards per catch—a phenomenal number for a tight end. He got invited to a post-season all-star game. He prepared for it like it was the Super Bowl, studying the playbook and rehearsing for his interviews with the professional scouts attending the game. From there, he was invited to the NFL Combine. He knew he wasn't going to blow anyone away with his bench press, so he focused on performing well in his interviews with coaches.

Eighteen months after his last basketball game, Julius suited up as a Denver Bronco. He started in a Monday

Night Football game against the Oakland Raiders, the team he followed as a kid in Stockton.

After seven seasons in the NFL, Julius retired and is now studying to be a performance psychologist. He'll focus on helping others achieve the most they can in life.

Does anyone doubt that he will succeed in this new pursuit?

THE APPROACH

You don't have to be a professional athlete to benefit from mental training and preparation. It works for everyone. Here are some suggestions.

Positive affirmations: Say what you want. Speak it into existence. Write down a positive affirmation or a statement that you can say every day. What do you want to see yourself achieve?

Visualization: Picture yourself succeeding in a meeting or when you have to speak in a public setting. Take five or ten minutes out of the day to see yourself as successful. You'll feel like you've already been there so when the moment comes, you're ready for it.

Breathing: Everyone knows taking a deep breath helps

you relax. But most people are breathing through their chest cavity when they should be breathing through their abdominal cavity. If you breathe through your abdominal cavity, your brain gets 30 percent more oxygen, and this clarifies your thoughts and improves your decision making. I use this kind of breathing on the sidelines because it keeps me in the moment and not thinking about the last play.

Meditation: I've done all types of meditation, from walking meditation to just sitting quietly in a chair. Find a technique that works for you and practice it. There's meditation using body scans, mindfulness, loving-kindness, and several others. Try a few and pick one that works for you. The goal is always to enjoy the moment and avoid judging whether the session was "good" or "bad." Stick with it and practice.

Whatever you do, respect the power of your mind. The mind is where our dreams and goals and imaginations flourish.

As kids on the playground, we counted down the make-believe game clock and pictured ourselves taking the final shot of the game. *This is for the win, folks!* We watched the ball drop cleanly into the net and then let the cheers wash over us.

That's our mind putting us in our dreams.

That's our mind picturing what we want.

Your mind is always going to be powerful. The mind makes life. It's what develops relationships.

It's what makes us human.

But to be a champion, you'll need to mix some hard work into your dreams. In the next chapter, we'll talk about the habits that help you do that.

CHAPTER SIX

SMALL STEPS LEAD TO BIG CHANGE

"Consistency: It's the jewel worth wearing; It's the anchor worth weighing; It's the thread worth weaving; It's a battle worth winning."

CHARLES SWINDOLL

"It's not what we do once in a while that shapes our lives. It's what we do consistently."

ANTHONY ROBBINS

In June of 2018, about a month before NFL training camps opened, I was doing drills with my trainer, Seth Minter. We practiced a five-yard drill that emphasized my acceleration step, which is the move you make to get the defensive back turned around.

Six months later, Seth posted a video of me in that week's game where I had two catches—both over twenty yards. He took the footage of me from the game and interspersed it with a video he shot back in June of me doing that drill.

My movements in both videos were identical.

In the game video, our opponent blitzed their corners and put the safety on me. I took the acceleration step, turned the safety around, and when I stopped and came out of my break, the ball was there. I saw the same thing in the drill video, except there, I took my steps on circles marked on the grass, and I made cuts around cones on the field.

I probably wouldn't have made the connection between the drill and the play. Still, when I watched the videos, I realized just how much my preparation in June was paying off for me six months later.

If you consistently practice your craft, each piece will fit together in an unstoppable package.

There's no luck involved. It's repetition.

It's practice.

TAKING YOUR FIRST STEPS

Consistency is key.

Consistency in your habits. Eat well. Get enough sleep.

Consistent training. Running. Weights. Stretching. Reading. Studying.

Steady mental preparation. If you use meditation or visualization, practice every day.

Make time for yourself as well as time for others. Make time for learning and self-improvement and always be on the lookout for habits that give you pleasure and help you get stronger, faster, healthier, and more resilient.

Decide what you love and what you want to do, and then make sure you spend at least a little bit of time every day to get better at that thing.

Practice.

Train.

Learn.

Every day.

It also pays to be consistent in your self-reflection. Accept that some things you try are not going to work. That isn't failure; that's learning.

Ask yourself: What are you doing at this moment that makes you feel secure and confident? If that approach works, keep doing it or remember to resume doing it when things start to go downhill.

Are you feeling adversity at this moment? Then ask yourself what it is that is making you feel that way, and decide to avoid the thoughts or actions that contributed to it. Consciously acknowledge what makes you feel powerful and what makes you feel weak, and learn to manage those feelings.

Know that you will have trials and errors and pitfalls.

Last year I encountered adversity and realized I was getting away from some things that had worked for me in the past. I asked myself: Why am I not playing well? What was I doing last season that made a difference?

You might be surprised by the answers you get when you ask yourself these questions. In my case, I realized I needed to get back on track with my visualization and prayer. When those things happen every day, things go well for me.

I don't believe the answer is to make big, sweeping changes. Minor adjustments can make all the difference. That's why coaches emphasize the details, the minute refinements that make your overall game better. Picture all those little things that contribute to your efforts, and you'll realize how they mesh and how each step contributes to your success. Missing just one of them can affect everything else involved.

Here are some tangible steps that will help you in this effort.

FIND PEOPLE TO EMULATE

Use those in your field who are outstanding, successful, and happy as models. What habits do they have that will work for you?

When I played with Demaryius Thomas, I tried to emulate aspects of his game. I'm writing this book in part because of my admiration for Peyton Manning, and I've always tried to model his mental toughness. I take things from a lot of people I encounter—not because I want to be like them but because they exhibit traits or habits that I admire. They will make me better at what I'm best at. These characteristics have made them successful, so I'm eager to try them out and see if they'll also work for me.

Emmanuel Sanders introduced this idea to me. When

I came to Denver as a rookie, he told me he was taking something from my game, and that he'd adopted things from Demaryius as well. He had no qualms about it, and I remember thinking, That's smart. You don't want to play just like those guys, but you *do* want to take certain things that they do well and fold them into your own game. It makes you that much more dangerous.

As the late German statesman Helmut Schmidt once said:

"The biggest room in the world is the room for improvement."

WRITE IT DOWN

Science tells us that when you clearly record your thoughts in writing, they become more indelible on the brain and trigger reaction. I started journaling earlier in my career when I first saw the need to improve. I wrote down my thoughts and included positive statements of things I wanted to happen. At first, they were minor things, like how I was going to have a great day or things that I really admired in myself. As I got into a routine, I wrote about broader aspirations and made more sweeping observations. I described practices and games—both the positive and the negative—and how I could improve.

Journaling helps relieve daily stresses. It makes you feel

better about yourself. You can relive events in a way that allows you to process them and learn from them without anxiety. You can use it to solve problems and clarify your thoughts and feelings.

IDENTIFY YOUR IMPROVEMENT GOALS

Look ahead to how you can improve. Even when I'm in midseason, I think about what I'll work on in the off-season. Since the prize is the journey, I'm always on my journey.

These are long-term goals and not things you need to fix right away. For instance, I know I want to develop a more consistent diet. I want to work on my speed. I want to work on my outside routes now that I'm no longer in the slot.

Polishing one area enhances others. If I upgrade my mental game, I elevate my physical game. If I hone my football preparation, I'll sharpen other aspects of my life. It all translates.

SELF-LOVE IS EVERYTHING

Dr. Rick Perea taught me the benefits of positive affirmations. Saying things like *I am confident, secure, and powerful* and *I believe in myself* programs your mind to accept this as fact. When you replace self-doubt with powerful, unambiguous assertions, your sense of well-being swells.

Dr. P helped me become more consistent with affirmations. I do positive self-talk every morning before I head into work and every night before I go to sleep. I've written my affirmations on cards. I go through them and say them with conviction.

This helps anyone who struggles with self-doubt. We all feel uncertainty—that's part of the makeup of the human mind—but these assertions diminish doubt and indecision. When self-esteem and confidence soar, these declarations have even more power. If you set goals, affirmations help you achieve them.

DEVELOP CONSISTENCY

As I pointed out in the last chapter, Dr. P stresses the value of having a process. What do you do every day to bring yourself closer to your goals? What do you do every day to succeed? Winning, he says, is a symptom of a good process, not an outcome.

Be clear about what you want. At Michigan State, I had teammates who could have played in the NFL but failed to catch on with a team. It wasn't a lack of physical ability that kept them out of the league; they simply didn't dream of playing professionally.

When you're clear about your goals, the best way to attain them is with a stable routine. For example, I write out to-do lists of things I'm going to work on. Some people tackle the easy stuff first, but I attack the most difficult things first because those activities require the most concentration and hard work.

DRILLS FOR THE FEET AND THE MIND

There is more to football than the average fan thinks. Highly skilled players break their technique down into subtle, discrete movements that, when reassembled, combine explosively.

I learned that from working with Seth Minter, aka "The Foot Doctor." Seth isn't an actual doctor, although I doubt there's a sports medicine textbook this guy hasn't read and absorbed.

But he's also more than a trainer. Seth challenges your assumptions and forces you to look at the world differently. He has ideas about past lives, alien abductions, and how the movements in football are not all right angles but more feminine in nature.

BELIEVING IN THE PROCESS

Dr. Rick Perea, performance psychologist

Coaches and scouts in the NFL don't understand the mental side of the game well. If they did, Bennie Fowler would have been a second-round pick instead of a free agent.

That's because Bennie is so dialed into the mental side of the game. His mental strength makes him stand out. Plenty of players are gifted physically, but mentally they don't have it going on. Bennie does. He's disciplined, focused, upbeat, and determined, and those are all vital qualities for anyone competing against the best players on the planet.

Look at Bennie. Undrafted free agent out of Michigan State. Good size, decent speed. But who is this guy? When he catches the ball, he immediately moves the ball upfield. Not sideways or backward but straight toward the endzone. He has a terrific internal drive. We call it a furnace, and Bennie has a big one that burns with a steady, hot flame.

I've worked with Peyton Manning, Tom Brady, and many of the top guys out there. Our walls are full of framed displays of their jerseys. I couldn't put up Drew Brees's jersey because we didn't have room.

But Bennie has a spot on our wall. It's a picture of him catching a ball against the Raiders and taking it upfield. I made space for Bennie because when people come into my office, I say, "Look at this kid. That's Bennie Fowler. He was an undrafted free agent who made it. I believe in him because he has used his mental strength and discipline to succeed. He believes he can do anything. He trusts the process."

Bennie's space on my wall is cemented.

I don't get to work as much with Bennie anymore now that he's no longer in Denver, but I know that Bennie continues to work on his own. Still, I miss him. He's a great football player, but more important, he's a great human being.

That's right: feminine.

"Everyday movement has a lot of curves," Seth told me once. "It's feminine, really. Nothing is a straight line. We move more like snakes than robots."

CLIMBING THE AGILITY LADDER

Seth grew up in Baltimore and was an outstanding athlete in football, baseball, and basketball. But football was his passion. He was a wide receiver. He might have played professionally if he hadn't torn his ACL in high school. Despite the injury, Seth played football at Bowie State, a Division II school in Maryland, and became the first person in his family to earn a college degree.

In college, Seth loved drills involving the agility ladder. He could no longer explode off his dominant left leg because of his previous ACL injury, but his footwork was phenomenal.

Seth admired Chad Johnson, a wide receiver from Oregon State who played eleven years in the NFL before retiring in 2012. Johnson was a devotee of footwork. He once said that football teams didn't pay him for his hands, but for his feet.

Seth watched a video Johnson made with Antonio Brown, Andre Johnson, and Santana Moss. The video showed the four NFL receivers running their routes and practicing their footwork around cones in the field. That video, combined with his own love of footwork, convinced Seth to develop a training program. He recorded and posted videos of his own drills.

Word got out. Athletes from his neighborhood started training with him. First, it was neighbors, then some high school athletes, and then college guys started calling him.

Then the call came from Ray Lewis.

Lewis, the All-Pro linebacker for Baltimore, heard about Seth from Juan Dixon, the former University of Maryland basketball star. Dixon recruited Seth to work with his cousin, a player in the Canadian Football League. Lewis watched videos and was blown away by how Seth approached footwork drills and training. Lewis had done and seen a lot of drills but nothing as specific and detailed as Seth's. Soon, players from around the NFL contacted Seth for help.

SOME UNCONVENTIONAL VIEWS

Seth believes each person has a unique set of muscular and psychological dysfunctions. So, he tailors training to account for that. In contrast, traditional training methods don't account for those traits. Conventional methods allow imbalances and systemic weaknesses to continue while throwing the added pressure of resistance training on top of it.

"What happens to pre-existing dysfunctions when you pile more resistance on top?" he asked me one day. "It makes it worse.

"I call it the death loop. You go into the weight room, and you get broken. Then you get sent to a physical therapist to get ready for surgery. The PT sends you to the surgeon, and you have the operation, and then the surgeon sends you back to the PT to recover from the surgery. When you're done there, the PT sends you back to the weight room to start the whole process over again. Am I the only one who sees that cycle happening over and over again?"

Seth says he's not welcome in some NFL training camps because of his outspoken views. Strength coaches and trainers don't like to hear that their methods are outmoded and hurt players. But the players are listening to him.

SETH'S PHILOSOPHY OF MOVEMENT

Seth's explanations for his work and ideas about human movement are often philosophical. He'll mention that the body has 137 trillion cells and that the key to success is getting each one involved and working synergistically. He calls this "omni-involvement."

He also believes we must search for our passion, even when we think we've found it. The universe is vast, and it always provides you with new situations. You can never think you have all the answers. What you see is what you permit the universe to show you. No one is deciding what you see. You determine that.

Two minutes into a conversation with Seth, you realize he questions everything and notices everything. When you're working with him, he raises questions such as, "How does a fetus's heart know to beat when the brain hasn't formed yet?" He works to develop your physical skills but also your mental abilities. Your heart, he'll tell you, is the real brain. Your brain is just trying to figure out what your heart is doing.

ALL IN ONE

Jaquail Jacox, agent

A big part of our work at All In One is keeping our clients motivated. We strive to keep their spirits high. When you play in the NBA or NFL, a lot of different obstacles come your way, and it helps to have a support system to help you navigate those things.

Here are some things I tell our clients about how to overcome adversity:

- **Cultivate a support network.** Much of the adversity players encounter can be kept in the right context when friends remind them of how great they are and how hard they've worked for their success. No one reaches the professional level without terrific natural gifts, good old-fashioned elbow grease, and friends who help them keep their perspective. At our company, we also take time to check on a client's well-being. Are you still eating right? Are you still training? Are you taking care of your body? This kind of thing helps guys stay sane when times are uncertain.

- **Stay positive.** Bennie is an excellent example of how to do this. He has a great outlook on life and tackles all his challenges in a clear-minded and purposeful way. A guy like Bennie stays ready for his next opportunity.

- **Set your sights on growth.** Don't be afraid to dream and picture what's next for you. We started out as a consulting company, but I wanted to be bigger. Today we do a lot more.

- **Dodge complacency.** I never want to lose my hunger for building my company, and this has taught me how important it is to maintain my drive every day. Hunger is not just a term; it's something you live by.

CHAPTER SEVEN

GOAL SETTING

"Ambition is a dream with a V8 engine."

ELVIS PRESLEY

"Keep away from people who try to belittle your ambitions. Small people always do that, but the really great make you feel that you, too, can become great."

MARK TWAIN

My long-term goal is to stay in the league for about twelve years. That goal reflects my confidence in the work I've done to be a receiver in the NFL.

But that isn't my only goal. I look beyond my career and think about evolving as a man and as a professional.

Life after sports.

I think of how people like Joe Dumars defined himself after playing professional basketball. Joe was the Detroit Pistons' president of basketball operations for many years. He earned the league's Executive of the Year award and becoming the first African American NBA general manager to win the NBA Finals. Today, Joe serves as a special adviser to the general manager of the Sacramento Kings.

Life and success did not stop for Joe after sports, and they're not going to stop for me. That's why I wrote this book. I want people to know I'm not just a football player. I want you to know that I achieved the highest level of play in the NFL because I am a complete person: flawed, determined, consistent, and perseverant. And my next successful journey will be forged by and indelibly linked to my mistakes, determination to overcome them, consistent work ethic to improve, and mental fortitude to go higher.

We all must continue to grow and evolve. To do that, you need specific goals, some of which can take years to reach. Guys like Terrell Davis or James Jones on the NFL Network prepared for life after football. So did Peyton. These guys are adapting, and so am I. I evolve every year. I get better at something every year as a player and as a person.

Any CEO in the country will tell you how crucial it is to have goals and to measure your progress toward those goals. Measuring your progress is the only way to keep your motivation and to know when you've achieved your objective. And then you repeat with new objectives.

Everyone in the NFL thinks about life after football. Everyone knows how quickly things change. Most players in this league at some point have been cut or had their careers threatened by injury. It's a way of life for us.

A CURVY ROAD TO SUCCESS

My friend Marell Evans played linebacker at the University of Michigan but declined offers to play professionally in Canada after college. Today, Marell is an operating partner with 415 Investments, a venture capital company in San Francisco.

Marell took a circuitous path to Silicon Valley. He grew up in Richmond, Virginia. His father died when he was four, and his stepfather died when he was twelve. Marell was raised by his mother, who worked three jobs to raise him and his brother.

Marell was the state player of the year in football in high school, and as a senior, he had about fifteen offers to play Division I football. He chose the University of Michigan and was the first person from his family to go to college.

Unfortunately, after his sophomore year at Ann Arbor, coaching changes and problems at home prompted Marell to leave Michigan. Oklahoma, Oregon, Virginia, Florida State, and other big schools called. Still, his family situation prompted him to quit college and work fourteen hours a day in a warehouse. He went from playing in front of 110,000 fans in Michigan to moving boxes in a Richmond warehouse. But he was able to set aside money to help stabilize his family's situation.

Eventually, Michigan lured him back. But even though Marell practiced every day with the team, he never earned enough credits to get into an actual game. Consequently, he never popped up on the NFL's radar. He was disappointed and sometimes depressed about how things had worked out for him.

But that didn't last long.

A NEW ROAD

Instead of lamenting lost opportunities in football, Marell threw himself into carving out a career in technology. He never majored in technology. He was a general studies student with average grades at Michigan. But that didn't hold him back.

Marell cultivated his relationships. He became close to

Dave Brandon, the former athletic director at Michigan. Brandon had been the CEO of Domino's Pizza and Toys R Us, and he encouraged Marell to pursue work in technology. "He told me, 'I think you can work in business,'" Marell said. "'I think you can use your story, your motivation, your intangibles, and everything you've created in sports to transition to business.'"

Marell contacted every technology company you can name—Google, Microsoft, IBM, LinkedIn. He applied at several top Fortune 500 companies. Eventually, he took an offer from IBM in New York because it had an accelerator program to help employees build skills in technology. He was the only black person in the program.

Surrounded by smart engineers, he realized his best option was to develop people skills, which many of the others in the program didn't have. He joined a Toastmasters Club. He brought his work presentations to meetings, and his group helped refine them. Soon, Marell was polished and confident.

His work paid off. He was promoted, and after a few years, he moved to San Francisco. He did not have a position lined up in the Bay Area, but he quickly found one. Eventually, he joined 415 Investments, which was founded in 2014 by Owen Van Natta and Grace Stanat and provides seed funding for and advises early-stage companies.

KEYS TO REACHING YOUR GOALS

Marell is a living example of what it takes to achieve your goals. Here are his three key steps to success.

FIND A MENTOR

You need an advisor who exhibits the qualities you'd like to see in yourself. Once you find this person, follow what Marell calls "the 80-20 rule." The 80-20 rule states that you need to spend 80 percent of your time listening to your mentor and 20 percent of the time speaking yourself and asking questions.

DON'T BE AFRAID TO BE DIFFERENT

Don't be afraid to venture into something that you aren't comfortable with, Marell told me. You won't be the first, and you won't be the last.

If Marell hadn't embraced his uniqueness early on, he might never have gotten his opportunity at IBM. When he saw that many of his colleagues didn't have confidence in their public-speaking skills, he slipped into that niche. "I didn't have the 'book smarts,' so I dedicated a ton of time to develop those skills, and it paid off," he told me.

'YOU'RE SO MANNERABLE'

Marell Evans

Bennie Fowler is one of the humblest people you could ever meet, and he's always been that way.

He asks me about my ideas and how I set goals, and I tell him, "Listen, Bennie. Things will work out for you because you treat people so well. You're so mannerable."

Bennie is a very hard-working person. To get to where he is after not being drafted is a real feat. The career prospects for undrafted players are always doubtful, but here's Bennie, a Super Bowl champion and in his fifth or sixth year in the league. He's already beaten the odds.

SURROUND YOURSELF WITH INCREDIBLE FRIENDS

Marell believes in that saying, "Show me your friends, and I'll show you your future." He feels your friends should be different from you. They should have different perspectives and backgrounds. But they should also be like you—hungry for success.

"I have white friends. I have Jewish friends. I have Indian friends," Marell told me. "I have a lot of different mindsets around me. I have a corporation of friends who are all different and bring different approaches to life. This corporation wouldn't run very well if everyone had the same strengths and outlook."

LITTLE SUCCESSES

Not all of your goals have to be grandiose. Don't get me wrong; you should have some big, overarching objectives. But you also need short-term targets that keep you moving toward your more far-reaching aspirations.

What works for athletes also works for those who aren't athletes. First, you have to visualize what you want to achieve and what you hope to be in your life. You can break this down in different ways. Career plans. Financial aspirations. Education. Family. Physical accomplishments. Maybe you have some artistic ambitions. Think about these things, and then select a few achievable goals in each category that make sense for you.

There is more than one path to success. In the next chapter, we'll talk about how to find happiness and success when you have to switch from Plan A to Plan B.

CHAPTER EIGHT

YOU DON'T HAVE TO BE AN ATHLETE TO MAKE A MILLION DOLLARS

"Lots of people want to ride with you in the limo, but what you want is someone who will take the bus with you when the limo breaks down."

OPRAH WINFREY

Some of my friends are professional athletes who have made millions of dollars in their sport.

But let's face it: most people are not going to make it to the pros. The competition is too fierce and talented, and the odds for most athletes are too long, no matter how hard you work at it.

I'm not saying you shouldn't chase your dreams. You should! If you want to be a professional athlete, by all means, pursue that goal with everything you've got. But, for athletes, don't think that just because you don't make it to the pros, that your athletic career is over. Recall the stories of Julius Thomas, Seth Minter, Marell Evans, and eventually the post-NFL story of me, Bennie Fowler. Find the unsolved problem in what you're really good at, and invest in *you*, the business that will last a lifetime.

My father was a great athlete who came close to playing professionally. But it didn't happen for him. Luckily, he grew up in a family culture that prioritized education, and he went on to a great career as an executive with Ford Motor Company. He always stressed the value of education.

In our society, making a million dollars is a metaphor for success. But how much money you make is a trivial way of keeping score. What's more important is your happiness. Are you doing what you love? Do you love going to work every day? Is what you're offering helping someone else?

Your Plan A might be to make it to the pros. That's a lofty target and shows how optimistic and confident you are.

Good!

But having a Plan B doesn't mean you're pessimistic. It doesn't mean you're not committed to Plan A. You're not allowing failure to be an option.

Plan B should make you feel great too. It can also be lofty and ambitious. It's smart to have a Plan B; it's not a sign of weakness.

For me, Plan B will be an offshoot of my Plan A. I have a network of friends, teammates, and advisors who will all be part of my Plan B.

Plan B isn't always dramatically different from Plan A. If your Plan A is doing something you love, make Plan B something you love too. Chances are it will involve the same friends and acquaintances you made while working on Plan A.

During the season, dedicate your efforts to being the best professional you can be. You don't want to be thinking about your Plan B at that time. But the off-season is different. That's time to dream and picture future options.

DRESSED FOR SUCCESS

One of my best friends in the world is Desyree Thomas,

the founder and CEO of Todd Patrick, a luxury menswear brand based in New York City. Like me, she grew up in Michigan playing a lot of basketball. She was a star at Division I Eastern Michigan and had aspirations to play professionally in Italy.

That never happened. But what *did* happen explains just how much courage and confidence play a role in someone's success.

Desyree and her little brother were raised by her mother in Waterford, Michigan, and whenever she faces a tough challenge, she thinks of how far she's come.

"The line people set for me was crossed a long time ago, so why should I pay attention to arbitrary limits?" she said.

"I've been adamant all my life about getting everything I felt I deserved in life. A lot of people who come from less-fortunate backgrounds have a mentality, *This is the hand I've been dealt* and they're OK with that. I was dealt a hand, too, but I asked for a reshuffle. That first hand wasn't good enough, and I wanted a new one. Driving my success is my adamant belief in going after what's mine."

Desyree truly lives this way. When her agent gave her an offer to play professionally in Italy, Desyree didn't think the offer was good enough. So she turned it down, moved to New York City, and carved out a creative niche in menswear instead. She started styling professional athletes, then launched her own company. Every garment in her line is hand-cut and sewn in New York. She created a fresh aesthetic, blending past styles and cultural influences to create a look that feels both new and traditional. That's my take on it. See for yourself at toddpatrick.co.

After basketball and before starting her clothing line, Desyree did some pro bono editorial work for fashion magazines and learned the business world of fashion. Sports and fashion were her passions. She contacted NFL players on social media and caught the attention of Rodney McCloud, a safety for the Eagles. She styled for him and then worked with Muhammad Wilkerson. Wilkerson is a six-foot-four, 315-pound defensive end with a size 44 waist. He has a hard time finding clothes that fit, let alone clothes that fit and look decent. When Desyree couldn't find clothes she wanted for these guys, she took free sewing lessons and made their clothes herself. Desyree found the uncaptured niche of an aspiring black female clothing designer who could talk sports while she perfectly and professionally outfitted the uniqueness of NFL athletes, and she moved this passion into a successful, growing fashion line.

She was ready to do anything to achieve what she was due.

But, as Draymond Green says, it's not what you *earn* that spells success, it's what you *do* with what you earn. In Desyree's case, what she did was name her new clothing company, Todd Patrick, after her little brother. Todd was living with their dad in Detroit—not in the "best situation," Desyree told me—and she wanted to show her brother something.

"I wanted him to know that it doesn't matter where we come from," she told me. "We can do anything we want. For instance, I can take your name and put it on every famous person in the world.

"As long as you're putting in this work and you're adamant about everything you feel you deserve, nothing else matters."

NETWORKING AND THE SUPPORT OF OTHERS

Everyone needs the support of their friends and other people, regardless of the profession they're in. It's all about who you know in this world and how strong those relationships are.

Do your teammates or colleagues trust and respect you? What would they tell others about you? Before the Patriots signed me, Bill Belichick called Peyton to find out what kind of player I was. The Giants signed me because my former coach in Denver was with the Giants and vouched for me. This underscores why you must give it your all, work hard, and be your best with others. You never know when an opportunity might spring from those relationships.

A WORD ABOUT PASSION

Desyree Thomas

People respect my work because they hear the passion when I talk about it. If you're not confident in yourself and what you can do, people will feel that.

How people value themselves determines how successful they will be. Bennie is a good example. On the field, he behaves like an elite athlete. He belongs there. You can hold yourself back if you don't value your abilities.

I met Bennie through Anthony Fields, who grew up with Bennie. I became close to Ant, and he told me, "You got to work with my boy, Bennie."

I started working with Bennie in 2016. Some athletes really don't pay much attention to what you're doing with your styling, but Bennie was different. He was hands-on and intrigued about the process of fashion and design. He was so intelligent about the things he wanted to accomplish that it further inspired me in my job with fashion. Bennie became one of my best friends.

Bennie makes me feel fortunate. When I first started, I felt that my vision and where I wanted to take athletes was different than anything I was seeing. Bennie helped me show what I can do.

In the NFL, people watch everything you do. They watch you in practice, at games, and on the sidelines. They watch how you interact with people.

If you're a person of high character, people remember that.

When we were young, my mother taught us that you never know who's watching you or listening to you. She taught us that when we go to work, we should dress nicely and neatly, speak clearly, and make sure people understand us. You are always making an impression on someone. In sports, coaches are not always looking at whether you scored. They are looking at how you support your teammates, take coaching advice, and act when things aren't going your way. When we became adults, my mother would say, "The person who's always watching you, should be you."

LESSONS FROM THE MOVERS

My friend Phil Harvey is an excellent example of how success emerges incrementally with small steps. About a decade ago, when Phil was twenty, he and his brother took jobs with one of the largest moving companies in the Denver area. They worked there for about eighteen months, and during that time, they learned as much as they could about the moving business. They noticed that their employer made a lot of mistakes. When the company started losing enough business to affect the Harveys' income, the brothers decided to go out on their own.

They started out using a Chevy Tahoe for every move. Not easy. When the Tahoe broke down, they borrowed a Ford Ranger from their mother and kept on working.

Phil and his brother, James, were excellent movers. They're both athletic, lean, and strong, and they make moving look easy. Their customers loved them and recommended them to all their friends. It wasn't long before they were making more working for themselves than they did working for a large moving company. Soon, they brought on a cousin to work with them, and he too became a partner in the business.

Over the next ten years, they built their business. Other avenues of income opened up for them:

- They started renting Budget trucks for their moves and then opened a Budget franchise so that they could rent vehicles from themselves.
- When they noticed that many clients requested carpet-cleaning recommendations, Phil's girlfriend started a side business for cleaning services.
- From carpet cleaning, they expanded again to offer

general cleaning for clients who were moving out of a rental or preparing their home for sale.

- When clients had them haul away unwanted furniture, the Harveys started a side business reselling the items on eBay.

Is there any angle that the Harveys missed? They can load and move someone's furniture and possessions. They can rent you a truck if you need one. They can haul off stuff you don't want. They can come in after the move and clean the carpet and the rest of the house. About the only thing they didn't do was sell the house when it was clean and empty.

Oh, wait. That's not true anymore. James recently got his real estate license. Now they can sell the house too.

REACHING YOUR GOALS

You should have big goals, but don't be limited by them. If your goal is to earn a million dollars, fine. But what's your goal after that? Setting a finite line can be delimiting, so you have to be nimble. Some defensive backs wanted to be wide receivers. They have similar body types and run as fast as receivers; they just don't catch the ball as well. But in the event the ball is thrown over the receiver's head, the DB, for the moment, can become a receiver with the interception. The DB achieved more than he had originally planned because he never limited himself to being just a tackler.

You should have goals for every month. You should have weekly goals. At Michigan State, Coach Dantonio handed out goal cards to us every week before the game. You were supposed to write down the five things you wanted to achieve that week, and then review it at the end of the week to see how you did. The process keeps you focused on getting better.

Vision boards are a big thing now. I understand why. People post their goals and put them in a conspicuous place. That way, the goal stays fresh in their minds. They're continually reminded to look forward and for ways to achieve that goal.

I made my first vision board the year we won the Super Bowl. I've also had vision boards on my phone. I've had dream books too. I did one of those in college, and I'm going to return to that practice this year. I'm repeating the principles I followed when I was the most successful. Returning to what works, works.

These tools serve as reminders of what got you to your high points. What path did you take up that mountain? Sometimes you have to remind yourself of the practices that brought you success so you can repeat them and keep them in your toolbox.

The 2018 season with the Giants was the most fun I've ever had in the NFL. Why was that? When I think back on that year and the habits I practiced, I realize that my visualization was on point every day throughout the season.

I'm not a big fan of dwelling on mistakes—they're over and done, and there is nothing you can do about them. You can't have that moment back no matter how hard you try.

But I do believe in reflecting on mistakes to determine their cause. *Where did I go wrong?*

Most of my mistakes result from taking shortcuts. One year, for instance, I started the season off very well. But then I had a couple of drops and my routes got sloppy. What was going on?

I quickly realized that I'd been cutting corners. I usually go to the team practice facility on my day off and catch extra passes. But during this period, I wasn't consistent about that. Some days I'd go and some days I wouldn't go. I'd miss a day and I'd think, I'll catch up later by doing extra when I have more time.

That approach doesn't work. Once you commit, you must be unwavering. It's easy to skip a day when you're having success. You think, Well, things are going well right now. I can afford to skip a day.

But you can't.

STAYING RESILIENT

Setting ambitious goals and steadily working toward them is just as crucial in business as in sports.

Marell Evans, who we mentioned in the last chapter, is an excellent example of this. Marell had an up-and-down college football career at the University of Michigan, and his dream of playing in the NFL never came to fruition. But he wanted a better life for himself after college, and he continued to work and build up his network.

Success depends on finding the things you are passionate about. Once you identify that, think about how you can be involved in that passion every day and how you can use your enthusiasm for that work to change the world. That's your sweet spot. You should do what you love and what you're great at.

THREE TIPS ON SUCCESS

Phil Harvey

A lot of young people ask me how my brother, cousin, and I managed to start such a successful family business. We started out ten years ago moving furniture with a little Ford Ranger truck. Today, we have a growing moving company with about twenty employees and several side businesses that dovetail with our moving company.

Here are three things I tell them about starting a new business:

- **Explore different options until you find something that you can be good at and that can make you money.** My brother and I didn't start our company until we had learned the trade while working for someone else. We learned that we enjoyed this kind of work, and knowing that prompted us to absorb everything we could learn about how to run a moving business.

- **Find a mentor.** After you figure out what you like, find someone who's already mastered the work and is willing to teach you what you need to know to get started yourself. You'll be surprised how generous successful business people can be—particularly with those who respect the work and appreciate the knowledge. I wish I had done this before we started our business.

- **Put in the time.** If you're looking to master something or to have great results, that takes time. It may take years of dedication. But if it's something you love to do (see tip number one), then you'll love this process, and the time will fly by.

Once you have your idea and your direction, look for partners who will complement your skills. In my situation, my two partners—my brother, James and my cousin, Dayyan Carter—have much different personalities than me. My brother is headstrong and a hard worker, but he's not the best with people. So he makes sure all our administrative things—like paying bills and setting up accounts—are taken care of. I'm diplomatic, so I'm in charge of the employees and scheduling. Dayyan is good with his hands, so he oversees the maintenance of our equipment and our trucks. We all have our roles, and we're all getting better at those roles.

CHAPTER NINE

LEADERSHIP

"If your actions inspire others to dream more, learn more, do more and become more, you are a leader."

JOHN QUINCY ADAMS

Steph Curry was taking questions from the media last year during the Golden State Warriors' training camp. It was day four of the camp, and you could hear the fatigue in Curry's voice. He was tired. And he was talking about leadership.

He was talking about Draymond Green.

"He's like the Energizer Bunny out there, even in practice," Curry said. "He doesn't let the intensity and vibe of practice drop. Like today. Day four of training camp, and you're tempted to back off a little, to let your body recover a little, and you might be a little sluggish. It's when you feel that way that you feed off the energy of the guys in practice, and Draymond is always that guy. As you go through this process, you need that kind of pick-me-up and that kind of consistency."

Anyone who's ever played with Draymond, including me, knows what Steph is talking about.

About a year later, when the Warriors were in Western finals, Draymond singled out the Warriors video coordinator, James Laughlin, for his leadership skills. Laughlin approached Draymond before the series opener and said Draymond needed to boost the confidence of the Warriors' bench players. The team would need those backups against the surging Portland Trail Blazers. Draymond said he took that advice to heart and paid particular attention to the Warriors' bench as a result.

Draymond is what his coach, Steve Kerr, calls the team's "emotional leader," and that's not because Draymond scores twenty-five a game and flushes theatrical dunks. Draymond leads the Warriors by demanding the most from his teammates and acknowledging anyone—including the video coordinator—who exhibits the team's core values of support and teamwork. Who else in the NBA takes time in a postgame press conference to praise a behind-the-scenes employee most fans have never heard of or care to know?

A true leader. That's who!

Next time you watch the Warriors play, study what Draymond is doing on the court. One second he is covering the opposing center (who's four inches taller), squaring up against him and forcing him to pass to a guard on the wing. In an instant, Draymond will switch from covering a seven-foot big man to covering a six-foot-three guard, reminding his teammates to "Move!" When the shot goes up, Draymond races to the block and grabs the rebound in front of the first guy he was covering. Then the outlet pass and the fast break. Don't be surprised if Draymond is filling one of the lanes of the fast break he initiated.

QUALITIES OF A GOOD LEADER

A good leader is fearless, and a good leader is not afraid to be wrong. Draymond's not perfect, but none of us are. That's why I called this book *The Imperfect Guide to Success*.

Peyton was another great leader. He probably still is, although he's retired and seems to spend his days traveling the country writing songs for Brad Paisley. But on a football field, he was fearless. He might have been wrong at times, but that didn't make him tentative.

Great leaders like Draymond and Peyton use their mistakes to learn and get stronger. They never let a mistake shake their confidence. Draymond, for instance, isn't the best player skill-wise on the Warriors, but they wouldn't win without his leadership. Anyone on the court with Draymond—whether it's Kevin Durant or a rookie from Fordham—knows Draymond is in charge and that Draymond will hold them accountable for doing their job. He's been that way since we played together on the same team back in our youth.

There are different leadership styles too. I'm not vocal, but I've always tried to lead by example. You lead by exhibiting the core values of your team. Training right. Eating right. Behaving respectfully. Caring about your teammates and looking for ways to help them both on and off the field.

Aqib Talib, the cornerback for the Miami Dolphins, is a great leader. Demaryius Thomas was a great leader by example and with words. Emmanuel Sanders leads by example. Peyton led by example and with his words. The way Peyton went about his business made you want to follow his example.

Great leaders are born with that ability, but you can refine those skills with practice. Draymond's silver spoon is his leadership ability. I'm sure Draymond has enhanced his leadership abilities with experience and by being around other remarkable leaders like Steve Kerr.

Someone like Draymond sees right to the heart of your motivation. When I listened to Steph Curry's comments about Draymond being an Energizer Bunny, I had to smile. I've worked out with Draymond many times, and he's a good leader even then. He'll say, "C'mon, Bennie! We need this! *You* need this! Remember what you're trying to achieve! This is how you get it! Show me that you want it."

And damn if he doesn't talk you into a few more reps, more pain...and a greater sense of mission and accomplishment. How do you say no to that kind of passion?

Aqib is like that. Peyton is the same way. Peyton would tell people, "I need more energy out here. This practice has got to get better!" You think guys rolled their eyes and faked it when Peyton said these things? No sir. You double down when your leader says things like that. Otherwise, you might find yourself jogging back to the huddle after a sloppy play and have him look you in the eye and say, "What type of shit was that?"

Something you never want to hear.

A RESPONSIBILITY TO LEAD

Many athletes learn about leadership in college. At Michigan State, Coach D expected seniors to have their best year. The program was built on that premise. Seniors were expected to lead by example in everything they did—in practice, with the media, in the locker room.

This encouraged many of us to become more vocal but also to more fully live the team's values and demand the same of the other players. Seniors have a responsibility to lead and bring their teammates together, creating the bonds and relationships that all great teams have. When I think back on that time, it's no surprise to me that we went 13-1 my senior year. I learned then that we all are public speakers. What you say or do can affect the next decision a person makes or the next move a person makes.

Olivier Vernon, the defensive end who was drafted out of the University of Miami, was a quiet leader when I played with him with the Giants. He didn't say much, but, like me, when he got on the field, he was all focus and execution. We both played with passion and purpose, and that provides leadership of a different sort.

Successful teams, like successful organizations, need different types of leaders. The best leaders, of course, are often the vocal ones. The Peyton Mannings of the world. Saquon Barkley, the running back for the Giants who played at Penn State, was a natural leader, even as a rookie. He led like a vet. He has a natural gift.

Even when they aren't playing well, or they're injured, great leaders stay involved and vocal. That might be the litmus test for leadership: how does this person handle adversity? Do they shut down and move to the back of the room? If that's the case, then they may not be a true leader.

A true leader takes their role seriously and plays that role regardless of their personal circumstances. They look for reasons to be optimistic during dark times. They see a swarm of problems as an opportunity to learn and grow.

That might be the most significant characteristic of a leader: they can reshape failure into inspiration and motivation not just for themselves but for their entire team. They are like Draymond, hovering over me while I bench press, shouting at me to give it more even though my muscles are burning.

Veteran players, like seniors at Michigan State, are expected to lead. For example, if you report to camp fat and out of shape, who is going to listen to you? Reporting to camp in poor shape is a sign that you're not preparing every day, that you're taking the job for granted, and that's no way to lead.

Playing in the NFL is a privilege that few people get to experience, and great leaders treat the opportunity with the respect it deserves.

At some point in your life, you will be called on to lead. It may not come in the form of standing before a group of young people hanging on your every word. Rather, it could be your young son or daughter coming home from school after failing a test. Or it could be as simple as looking at yourself in the mirror one morning and mouthing the words, "What's the damn point?" You have the responsibility to conjoin emotion with reason and process, and will yourself and whoever's listening to the next step forward.

PUTTING IT ALL TOGETHER

I've thrown a lot of ideas at you in this book, and I've introduced you to some amazing individuals.

But whether we are talking about a training expert from Baltimore, a clothing designer from New York, or a venture capitalist from Silicon Valley, a few clear messages stand out for anyone who is interested in success.

- **Find your passion.** Discover what you love and can do better than anyone else. This is your wheelhouse and focusing on it can transform you into a superstar. Keep searching for your passion even after you think you've found it; as my friend Seth Minter says, the universe is huge. It will provide new situations if you are open to them. You can never think you have all the answers.

- **Never stop learning.** Read widely and look for fresh ideas to expand your understanding of yourself and the world around you. Keep evolving and improving.
- **Respect yourself.** When you step out on the field or into the boardroom, behave like you belong there. Remember what my friend Desyree says: how people value themselves determines how successful they will be. So, trust your intelligence and your abilities, and don't let doubts hold you back.
- **See setbacks as assets.** We all face adversity, regardless of our backgrounds. Those who succeed are those who see setbacks as an opportunity to learn more and improve. They don't waste time wallowing in self-doubt or pity; they use failure to motivate them to get better.
- **Set specific goals.** If you don't know what you want, how will you know when you arrive? Set goals. Set big goals but also little goals and measure the progress you make in reaching them. And reevaluate your goals from time to time. Are they still challenging enough? Can you reach even higher? Challenge yourself.
- **Choose your friends wisely.** Surround yourself with people who will support you but also challenge you. Look for a diverse circle of friends—people who think differently about the world than you do who can open you up to ideas you wouldn't have otherwise consid-

ered. Seek out people who are willing to challenge your assumptions and perspective on the world and force you to look at life from a different angle. Find mentors and admirable people to emulate. You are the corporate leader of your life; employ friendships that will advance all in the corporation.

- **Practice discipline.** I say "practice" because no one has fully mastered discipline. The second you think you have mastered it is the moment that you should realize you still have a lot of work to do. Self-mastery never ends, so make it an enjoyable process. Keep a journal. Meditate. Visualize. Speak positive affirmations. These are all tools of self-discovery.
- **Help others.** None of us has gotten to where we are without someone's help, and in that sense, we have what I would consider an obligation to find ways to help those who need it. Think of it as another way to learn and improve as a person.
- **Train body and mind.** Just as you work to build your strength, speed, and flexibility, you need to train your brain. Learn to quiet your mind by sweeping out negative thoughts and replacing them with positive, uplifting thoughts. Learn to tap into that parasympathetic side that relaxes your muscles, fosters confidence, and leads to outstanding performance.
- **Work before you play. Because my mom said so.**

Each play in football involves hundreds of discrete and

disparate actions unspooling simultaneously on a flat patch of turf. Twenty-two players, each with their own assignment but also with their own ideas about what success looks like. Some move with intense, practiced concentration while others move as if on instinct. These plays last about four seconds. Then we all jog back to our places and do it over again, only this time with different actions and perhaps different motivations.

For me, that microcosm brings great joy. Even in defeat, most football players would agree that those brief moments are like vials of distilled passion, and we feel privileged to get a sip.

I know football for me is not going to last forever. Not many people can play into their thirties and forties—the sport's too demanding for long careers.

What's next?

I love talking with people. I get along with people, and people like being around me. I have a story to tell. So, where will that lead me?

Well, for starters, I could write a book! I've certainly enjoyed this process. I've enjoyed bringing in the stories of all the great people who've had an impact on me. Each of them has inspired me in ways that are both profound and reassuringly simple. It's been an enormous pleasure to bring them along with me on this journey.

The journey.

The prize.

Mike Sadler, my late friend and the punter on our college team, was so right: the prize is the journey. The journey will be imperfect and will definitely have its highs and lows. Your gift, your silver spoon, will bring perspective, calm the stormy seas, and prepare you for more. The prize is what you discover along the road. The prize is not the destination, because once you learn the value of challenging yourself, improving yourself, training yourself, and learning about yourself, you never want that journey to end.

ACKNOWLEDGMENTS

Thank you to all of my family, friends, and teammates; my parents, Bennie Fowler and Teresa Gueyser; and everyone who has helped me succeed, on and off the field.

ABOUT THE AUTHOR

BENNIE FOWLER is a wide receiver in the National Football League. He won a Super Bowl as a member of the Denver Broncos, where he caught legendary quarterback Peyton Manning's last professional pass, a two-point conversion at the end of that championship game. Known for his incredible work ethic and discipline, Bennie has devoted as much time to honing the mental aspects of the pro game as the physical. His insights into what it means to be a success in life have implications no matter where you find yourself in life's pursuits.

CPSIA information can be obtained
at www.ICGtesting.com
Printed in the USA
FSHW020223290120
66582FS